The
# FUNDAMENTALS
## of HOGAN

## by DAVID LEADBETTER
### with LORNE RUBENSTEIN

*SLEEPING BEAR PRESS*
*Chelsea, Michigan*

McCLELLAND & STEWART
*The Canadian Publishers*

Sleeping Bear Press
The Clocking Tower Building
Third Floor
310 North Main Street
Chelsea, MI 48118

McClelland & Stewart Ltd.
*The Canadian Publishers*
481 University Avenue
Toronto, Ontario
M5G 2E9

Canadian Cataloguing-in-Publication Data
Leadbetter, David
            The fundamentals of Hogan
ISBN0-7710-7850-1
1. Hogan, Ben, 1912-1977..2. Swing (Golf). I. Rubenstein, Lorne.
II. Title.
GV979.S9L42 2000              796.352'3           C99-930745-2

McClelland & Stewart acknowledges the financial support of the Government of
Canada through the Book Publishing Industry Development Program for their publishing activities. They further acknowledge the support of the Canada Council for
the Arts and the Ontario Arts Council for their publishing program.

Ben Hogan photographs from this book can be purchased from Golf Links to the
Past, official licensee of the Ben Hogan Golf Company. Contact them at 800-449-
4097 or visit www.golfpast.com

Published by arrangement with Sleeping Bear Press, Chelsea, Michigan, and
Doubleday, a division of Random House, Inc., New York, New York.

Printed and bound in the United States of America

1 2 3 4 5 04 03 02 01 00

Like many golfers, I have always enjoyed reading instructional books. As a youngster I found myself so fascinated with reading what Arnold Palmer, Jack Nicklaus and Gary Player, the big three, as they were known, had to say about the swing that I often slipped a golf book inside the cover of a Latin textbook during school. The game of golf really intrigued me—far more than the ancient Romans did. Eventually I turned professional at the age of eighteen. I continued to read and experiment at every opportunity while I played tournaments and also while I taught the game at the club where I was working. I was curious about how one author adhered to a particular idea while another would state what seemed to be the exact opposite—yet each writer put forward a solid case for his theories. For me, golf books and learning about the swing were endlessly fascinating; I was barely through a new idea before I would go out to try it. Sometimes I even did this after work, with my car's headlights on. By now I've amassed a library of instructional books, and still enjoy referring to them and studying them. My office at home is full of instructional books wherever I look, and I often find myself reaching for one, almost absent-mindedly, because, I suppose, there's always something to learn. It might be something that six-time British Open champion Harry Vardon wrote; or an idea from the work of Bobby Jones, Byron Nelson, Ben Hogan, Sam Snead, Nicklaus, or Tom Watson. The compelling aspect of golf to me is that, as long as I've taught the game, I'm still learning about it.

Of all the books in my library, Hogan's have absorbed me the most. I was always aware of his reputation as a consummate ball-striker, and so I turned to his writings with great interest. I wanted to find out what the master said, whether he was writing in magazines, in his first book *Power Golf*, or his classic *Five Lessons: The Modern Fundamentals of Golf*. I have reread Hogan's writings many times, and have learned so much from them. I've analyzed his work endlessly, or so it seems to me. I continue to think about Hogan's ideas and to learn from them. I have also adapted some of Hogan's ideas while developing my own. I have examined from many angles what Hogan had to say.

In particular, I have had a deep and abiding interest in *Five Lessons*, which began as a series of lessons in the magazine *Sports Illustrated*. This book was the direct result of Hogan working on his own swing. Hogan was relentless in his pursuit of a correct, powerful, and repeating swing, and he eventually achieved that goal. He tested his swing in the ultimate crucible of competition at the highest levels—the major championships—and found that it stood up. Hogan won two Masters, four United States Opens, one British Open (the only one he entered), and two PGA Championships, all between 1946 and 1953. No wonder he felt he had something to contribute to the game through the written word.

After Hogan was satisfied that he'd built a swing he could depend on under pressure, he was ready to write *Five Lessons*. The book began as a series of five articles that *Sports Illustrated* published in 1957. In June 1956, the magazine had sent its golf writer Herbert

Warren Wind, along with the illustrator Anthony Ravielli, to meet Hogan in his hometown of Fort Worth, Texas. Hogan at first had only one instructional article in mind on, as Wind later wrote, "the basic elements of the correct golf swing." But Wind and Ravielli asked Hogan if he would consider a series of articles on the steps he would suggest to a golfer willing to work steadily on his swing so that he could improve. Hogan liked the idea, and the threesome worked on the project at the Colonial Country Club in Fort Worth. A second meeting took place in early January 1957, and the first of five articles was published in *Sports Illustrated* in its March 11, 1957 issue. The five installments in the magazine became *Five Lessons*, which was published later that same year.

*Five Lessons: The Modern Fundamentals of Golf* differed in both content and presentation from Hogan's first book, *Power Golf*, published in 1948. *Five Lessons* has been a golfing bible for many players of all levels. Every tour player with whom I'm acquainted has read the book. Mark O'Meara, the 1998 Masters and British Open champion, first met Hogan in 1980. O'Meara had won the 1979 United States Amateur using Hogan clubs. He signed with the Hogan equipment company to play its clubs after he turned professional, at which time Hogan told him during their first meeting that he had learned the swing piece by piece, having thought about it night after night, and then trying out his ideas the next day on the practice tee. Hogan kept what worked and discarded what proved inadequate to his plan of building a reliable swing. O'Meara never forgot their conversation, and built his own swing segment by segment.

We can also think in this context of Larry Nelson, one of the most consistent players of the modern era. Nelson did not take up golf until he was twenty-one years old, having read *Five Lessons* closely. He used the book as a manual to help develop his technique and went on to win the 1983 U.S. Open and the 1981 and 1987 PGA Championships. *Five Lessons* has influenced golfers since the day it was published; the book still sells forty years after its original publication.

In my case, *Five Lessons* was one of the first instruction books I owned and read while growing up. The design of the book, quite apart from the elegantly expressed text, demonstrates all the organizational qualities and attention to detail that epitomized Hogan's character. The book was certainly a classic and in my opinion was way ahead of its time. It became the benchmark for future instruction. It is also a deeply personal book in that it reflects Hogan's attempts to deal with his own questions and provides the answers that he found. Many instruction books that professional golfers write are personal in similar ways.

I have for some years wanted to evaluate *Five Lessons* and some of Hogan's other writings from the perspective of what we have learned about the golf swing since Hogan's analyses. It seemed fortuitous, then, when I received a call in 1998 inviting me to do just that. The publisher of this book had located and secured the rights to previously unpublished photographs that Ravielli took as source material for *Five Lessons*. He wondered if I might be interested in examining these photographs and Hogan's writings. I looked at the photographs and was struck by the fact that here we had Hogan posing for the pictures. He was obviously well aware of the details of his swing because he was posing in dozens of different positions. In some cases the poses represented what he did at speed and in other cases they represented what he thought he did during the swing. I was immediately reminded of a phenomenon I have so often seen in my teaching and that is applicable to all golfers: the difference between "feel and real."

The discovery of these photographs led directly to this book. I felt a rush of excitement when the opportunity to write it presented

Herbert Warren Wind, Ben Hogan, and Anthony Ravielli.

itself, and although I had all but mapped out my entire year, I knew instantly that I wanted to begin work on this book. It was an opportunity not to be missed. To have located Ravielli's photographs is in golfing terms an unprecedented archaeological find. I also feel fortunate to have worked with illustrator Keith Witmer on this book. Keith has a deep appreciation for the nuances of Ravielli's work and also of Hogan's technique.

It was a great stroke of luck to find Ravielli's photographs. Any Hogan artifact is a priceless commodity, as there is not an abundance of pictures or film of him compared to the wealth of material available on today's top players. I am thrilled to have had the opportunity to study Ravielli's photographs and to spend so much time with Hogan's book again. This book, *The Fundamentals of Hogan*, is the result of that process.

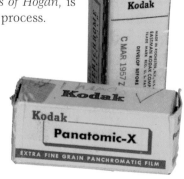

The original film Ravielli used to capture Hogan's swing.

# ACKNOWLEDGMENTS

When I was approached to write this book, I realized I would need the help of a writer who both knew the golf swing and who was familiar with Ben Hogan's theories. I had spoken many times over the years with Lorne Rubenstein, and had read the book he had written with Nick Price as well as the one with the late George Knudson. I was also familiar with his writings on golf in many publications, and felt he and I could work well together. Lorne's interest in technique and the history of the game, along with his research abilities, made him an ideal writing companion.

Lorne and I have spent many a late night/early morning on the telephone, changing, refining, and fiddling with the text. It seemed a never-ending quest that I suppose is similar in nature to the golf swing—you work at it, you leave it, you change it, always hoping it's going to get that little bit better. Finally we decided that it was time to go out to play, and let people read what we had written.

I hope that you, the golfing public, will enjoy reading this book as much as Lorne and I have enjoyed writing it (although we didn't always feel that way at one o'clock in the morning). I hope the work we put into it shows, because we spared no effort in trying to make this book helpful to all golfers. I would like to thank Lorne for his untiring work and patience, and hope his golf game has not suffered too much as a result. He made my job a lot easier.

To our fine, talented artist Keith Witmer, whose illustrations added so much to this book—thank you for your perfectionism.

Thanks also to various members of my staff who participated in getting this book to press. You all helped tremendously.

I also appreciate the help that various readers of the manuscript offered as it took shape. Most especially I thank Harvey Freedenberg, a lawyer and golfer who clearly is a serious reader. Harvey, I think, could easily make the move from law to editing.

A special word of thanks goes to Curtis Gillespie, who edited the manuscript and whose suggestions were invaluable. And, of course, a word of appreciation to our publisher, Sleeping Bear Press.

My thanks and love go to my wonderful family—my wife Kelly and our children Andy, Hally, and James. They unselfishly urged me to write the book and supported me all the way. I couldn't have completed this book without them.

And finally, I'd like to address all the golfers out there—amateurs and professionals alike—who have challenged me to guide them toward golfing bliss. Your feedback has been invaluable in helping me become a better teacher and communicator.

Hogan was constantly thinking about his technique.

If you were to ask today's tour players to vote on the best ball-striker of all time, the vast majority would pick Ben Hogan. They would place him at the top of the list even though many of them never saw him hit a shot. But so mighty is the reputation of the man that his name remains synonymous with pure ball-striking. The English writer and course architect Donald Steel observed that Hogan "was an extreme perfectionist and a ruthless competitor. His control was absolute, his dedication immense. He was the finest stroke player the game has known, a legend in his lifetime." Indeed, he is a legend beyond his lifetime; since Hogan died in 1997, his legend has only grown. Today, when a golfer controls the flight of the ball and moves it around the course at will, we say "You're hitting it like Hogan." There is no higher compliment. Ben Hogan remains the standard of excellence.

Hogan's reputation as the game's preeminent ball-striker could well last as long as the game is played. At the same time he could be called the father of modern golf instruction—in which the basic idea is that the player is to use the big muscles of the body, rather than the hands, as the controlling influences in the swing. Nobody has influenced modern-day teaching more than Hogan. His years of observation, his unceasing trial-and-error experimentation that he put to the test in championships, his love for hitting practice balls, and his unwavering desire for perfection, led him to become the most precise golfer in the annals of the game. Hogan was the consummate practicer and tinkerer, and enjoyed working on his technique at every opportunity. He would use any location in his pursuit of swing perfection: driving ranges and fields en route to a tournament, hotel rooms, locker

1

The locker room practice session!

rooms—any place where he could swing a club.

Hogan is truly a legend—one of the game's most esteemed players. Yet many observers did not consider Hogan to be a natural player in the same vein, for instance, as his archrival Sam Snead. He worked extremely hard to achieve his results precisely because he wasn't a natural player, making several dramatic changes to his swing over the years. Hogan's own efforts and results proved to him that it was indeed possible to improve by working on fundamentals. In Hogan's case, his hard work culminated in his finding, by 1946, his so-called "secret," a formula to eliminate the persistent hooking problem that early on threatened to ruin his development as a tournament player. This gave him complete mastery over the golf ball and allowed him to play the commanding golf for which he became famous. It was during the next seven years that he won his nine major championships.

Hogan's ability to change his swing was impressive. Every golfer who has tried to modify his swing knows how formidable a task it can be; one's instincts and habits always seem ready to show up again under pressure no matter how hard one works. Every golfer is different and every swing has its own look, which is why one can readily identify a player from a distance as he swings.

Hogan, too, had his personal look, and during his ruthless self-examination he learned that he was prone to a loss of control for specific reasons. His great flexibility caused him to swing the club back a long way and gave the impression that he had a fairly wristy swing, which, when combined with his fiery leg action, led to his early tendency to lose control of the clubface through impact and to hook the ball. But finally one could candidly state that for a period of time Hogan mastered the game and overcame his few bad tendencies—by finding and incorporating the small number of fundamentals which allowed him to develop a

repeating, effective swing. This mastery enabled him to manage his game so that he could plot his way around a course like a chess player; no fairway was too narrow and no pin was inaccessible. His course management and attention to detail were second to none, and his scores showed it. One might point to his play while winning the Masters, United States Open, and British Open in 1953 as proof of the soundness of his swing theories; he dismantled an extremely difficult Carnoustie in Scotland that year while winning the British Open with descending scores of 73-71-70-68. Hogan learned a little more every day about how to play the course. He had the tools—the refined, simplified technique—to dissect the challenging links. *The Daily Telegraph* newspaper asked after his victory: "And who shall say he's not the best of all time?"

As serious a student of the game as Hogan was, he did not have the luxury of using high-speed sophisticated video cameras or computers to analyze other swings or his own. He remarked in his later years that had he had such equipment he would have understood the swing ten years sooner. He also did not

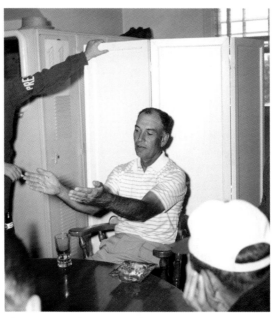

When Hogan spoke, everyone listened.

Working with Herbert Warren Wind on *Five Lessons*.

Hogan was a superior athlete, gifted with remarkable flexibility and range of motion, as well as an imaginative mind. According to many people, his intellect bordered on genius. Gardner Dickinson, a professional golfer who won three tournaments on the U.S. tour from 1968-1970 and played on two Ryder Cup teams, worked as an assistant to Hogan when he was briefly the head professional at the Tamarisk Country Club in Palm Springs, California during the early 1950s. Dickinson held a degree in clinical psychology and was qualified to administer psychological tests. He could not prevail upon Hogan to take a standard intelligence test, but did slip in some questions during their conversations. He estimated that Hogan's I.Q. was in the high genius category.

Combine Hogan's inherent qualities with his intense concentration and steely focus, and it is apparent he always had the foundation to become one of the game's finest players. Hogan had the strength, speed, and agility that are ideal for taking up the demands of golf. He had fairly long arms relative to his height (he stood 5 feet 8½ inches), with a powerful, compact body; at the height of his career he weighed in the region of 140 pounds, and every pound seemed there for one purpose—to strike the golf ball efficiently. He also had big hands and very strong forearms, which helped him hold on to the club with control and power from start to finish. I also believe that his powerful lower body, in particular the strong gluteus maximus muscles (buttocks) and thighs aided his superb stability—a major factor in enabling him to go at the ball hard while retaining perfect balance.

have a full-time coach as most players do today, although Hogan did on occasion confer with the renowned professional Henry Picard. But his uncanny sensory system, his powers of observation, and his tremendous kinesthetic awareness of how his body and the golf club functioned during the motion of a swing provided the underpinnings of his education. His greatest success occurred when he developed total belief in his technique so that he could play without worrying about bad shots. His relentless pursuit and eventual achievement of building a correct, powerful, and repeating swing that he could depend on under pressure led him to write *Five Lessons*. Hogan's book was published four years after he won those three majors in 1953. It is, as I have noted, a deeply personal book. It is a book about Hogan's search for a better swing for himself, and in it—having written *Power Golf* and in a variety of other publications—he offers his conclusions about what all golfers can learn from his own quest. His teachings have so much to offer golfers, but it has always been important that readers interpret his ideas correctly and clarify them properly. I hope to help with this.

Having been fortunate enough to be involved in the teaching side of golf for years and having taught some of the world's great modern players, I regard the writing of this book as a labor of love and joy. It is an honor for me, but moreover it is a tribute to a man that I, along with millions of others, have long admired and respected. Many younger golfers have heard of Hogan but perhaps do not realize he was the ultimate technician of the swing, and that he had more control of the ball than anyone who has played the game. Many good players like to draw the golf ball, but some of the greats prefer to fade it; that was true of Hogan, and it is also true of Jack Nicklaus. In Hogan's day, players had such immense respect for him that they would stop their own practice sessions and gather to watch the master at work. Though Hogan was basically a quiet man, even taciturn, when he talked about the golf swing players listened intently. Tommy Bolt once said that he remembers Jack Nicklaus watching Hogan practice, but that he never saw Hogan watching Nicklaus. Bolt meant this not as a slight to Nicklaus, but as a statement about Hogan's reputation and exalted place in the game.

My goals in this book are threefold: (1) to examine what Hogan believed about the swing; (2) to offer my interpretations and, in some cases, examine his thinking as expressed primarily in *Five Lessons*, but also from other sources, so that I might provide a complete picture. Hogan wrote the aforementioned *Power Golf*, and also in such publications as *Life* and *Esquire*, and of course he wrote for and was often quoted in golf magazines. In regard to his many writings I will attempt to clear up some misconceptions that have arisen over the years. Speaking from experience, I am aware that misconceptions can easily arise when dealing with the complexities of the golf swing; and (3) to offer advice that could help golfers of all ability levels who dream of shooting 80 or lower; not so that golfers can recreate Hogan's swing—that would be impossible—but so that they can learn from him and incorporate certain elements into their games and so become more consistent. Hogan believed that the golfer who studied and understood the basics of the swing and who then applied these principles in practice could develop a consistent swing and break 80. I also believe this.

On the subject of breaking 80, I think it is important to realize that this is indeed a dream

for many golfers—a dream they hope to turn into reality. An improved golf swing will go a long way toward achieving this goal. At the same time, we should never forget how important it is to work on your short game and develop it in tandem with your long game. Hogan did not address the short game in *Five Lessons* nor will I do so here. But an improved short game is vital to any golfer's plan to reach his potential. Ideally this book will help you improve your swing so that you do not have to tinker with it every time you practice. You will, I hope, be able to use your practice sessions to maintain your newfound, reliable swing and to devote more time to your short game. When I visit golf courses I see people beating golf balls hour after hour in hopes of improving their swings, although frequently they are working without a plan or concept—and they rarely work on their short games. This is understandable because they hit the ball poorly and are motivated to find something, anything, on the range.

I hope to give you that "something" in these pages, and in doing so free you to spend more time on your short game. This should help you become a consistent 80-breaker; or if you are already at that stage, a par-breaker.

I might add that I think along lines similar to Hogan in many important ways and consider myself something of a traditionalist when it comes to teaching the swing. I have always believed that no golfer can make headway in the game without understanding the fundamentals; the idea is then to stick with and work at these fundamentals. If in tandem you can develop a good short game, then you may well turn that dream of breaking 80 or breaking par into reality. This is one reason I am excited by the prospect of helping to bring Hogan again to the forefront of golfers' minds, and ensure that he remains there. I consider this book a conversation with Hogan about his theory of the swing, and a blending of what we have learned about it and what we can hope to achieve in further study. It's a blending, in other words,

Stability and balance were major factors in Hogan's swing.

of the past and present with an eye to the future.

As much as this book is an opportunity for me to engage with Hogan's thinking, I am at the same time reminded that I never saw the man strike a ball. This is my one big regret in golf. On one occasion my friend and student David Frost, who was on good terms with Hogan and represented the Hogan company, set up a time for me to watch him hit balls at Shady Oaks, his club in Fort Worth. Regrettably, Hogan became ill and my visit was canceled. Still, in the course of writing this book I do feel that in a way I encountered Hogan. My research led me to speak with many people who knew him and his game, and to examine every bit of information available about Hogan, including books, films, and letters. I feel I have come to know him—not only his swing but to some extent what made him tick—and I can only say I have more admiration for the man now than ever before.

It is interesting to note that while Hogan said years after writing the book that he put everything he knew about the swing into it, still he felt that there was more to learn. Hogan, in fact, encouraged further study and interpretation by declaring in *Five Lessons*: "I hope that these lessons will serve as a body of knowledge that will lead to further advances in our understanding of the golf swing. Every year we learn a little more about golf. Each new chunk of valid knowledge paves the way to greater knowledge. Golf is like medicine and the other fields of science in this respect." Nick Price, with whom I have had the good fortune to work for years, feels that he could compress twenty-five years of learning into just a couple with the information available today. The pace of learning is accelerated and compressed today; all golfers including those who have played for decades can benefit from the advances in teaching.

I might also point to Nick Faldo, with whom I started working in 1985. Faldo wanted to rebuild his swing so that he could rely on it under the pressure of major championships. It took him two years to incorporate the changes, and in 1987 he won the British Open after making eighteen straight pars during the final round—proof that his swing could stand up under extreme pressure. He has since gone on to win two more British Opens and three Masters. I learned while working with Faldo that it really is possible for a golfer to revamp his swing, as Hogan suggests it is. Clearly, not all golfers want to put in the time that Faldo did, because he is, of course, a touring professional, cast in the Hogan mold of dedication. Still, as Hogan points out, any golfer who is committed to change can improve as long as he works on the fundamentals. Faldo, like Hogan and now Tiger Woods, has been driven by the search for perfection. Your own search might be so that you can work toward winning a club event, or simply to reach a new personal best in terms of ball-striking and scoring. Hogan believed it and I believe it: you can improve. Just as I was amazed to see the changes in Faldo over time I have been equally amazed to see the changes in amateurs with whom I have worked, though not at all surprised to observe how much they have enjoyed their golf as a result.

Hogan's ideas provide an extraordinarily valuable resource for our continued studies. *Five Lessons* especially is a constant and consistent companion to many golfers, teachers, and players. Nick Price has read and reread and marked up the book with comments and observations; there are places he agrees with Hogan and occasions where his opinions differ. I plan to do something similar here. I will, in a sense, mark up *Five Lessons* and examine it from our turn-of-the-century perspective. I hope I can accomplish this act of interpretation judiciously and with the respect it requires. I would also encourage you to read or reread *Five Lessons*—Hogan's swing theory becomes that much clearer.

The idea, of course, is to help you work toward developing a reliable swing. The more reliable your swing, the more you can trust it, and the greater your confidence. The chances of your building this confidence will be enhanced when you feel secure with what you are doing; this security will come when you incorporate the correct fundamentals so that you can produce a reliably effective swing and control the distance, direction, and trajectory of the ball. The mental side of the game, including course strategy, becomes that much easier. The idea is to know where the ball will and won't go. The golfer has to realize that every shot won't be perfect: the key is learning to hit "better bad shots," keeping the ball in play through sound mechanics—basically, believing in your technique, making it subconscious and instinctive through practice so that you can go out on the course to simply play the game.

When you reach this point you have achieved the ultimate—you can think about quality practice sessions in terms of just maintaining and refining your technique and then hitting different types of shots for pure enjoyment—for example, draws and fades, high and low shots. You will then have plenty of time left to practice that all-important short game. You certainly don't have to be like Ben Hogan in your practice habits; however, making good use of your time and practicing with a purpose will go a long way toward your shooting lower scores.

I base some of the key building blocks in my teaching upon Hogan's fundamentals: grip, setup, plane, the lower body motion, the basic use of the big muscles, the understanding of the action of the hands and arms, the use of physics to strike the ball, the application of drills and mirror practice to learn technique. His influence is plain to see in my teaching. I based my first book, *The Golf Swing*, on the style and layout of *Five Lessons*. Hogan's book is, I feel, the first systematic approach to

teaching the full swing, a step-by-step guide to help a golfer understand the components of the swing and then to put them all together.

Even though he wrote his book in the 1950s, much of what Hogan said, when examined closely, holds true today, so it is no surprise that *Five Lessons* is a focal point of every serious golfer's library. It has played a major role in the evolution of teaching the game. Like Hogan, I believe that many golfers are simply spinning their wheels and not improving. Hogan himself once spun his own wheels. In an article in *Esquire* in 1942 called *"When Golf Is No Fun,"* Hogan wrote that he had taken the same sort of punishment that struggling amateurs know all too well.

"Before I really found my game," Hogan wrote, "I might be hot one round and cold the next for no reason I could figure out. After rounds when I wasn't scoring well I would practice for hours trying to get to hitting the ball, and finally go home disgusted."

But Hogan wouldn't tolerate that feeling, so he studied the golf swing carefully with an eye to eliminating his sources of error and making it efficient and reliable. He was able to do this, and came to believe that with the proper understanding and application of the fundamentals and with patience, everyone has it within his or her grasp to play good golf. Hogan is right when he says, "Doing things the right way takes a lot less effort than the wrong way does." I agree, and invite you to examine the following pages with a view to learning to build a reliable and efficient swing. I am confident you will be on the way to reaching your potential when you understand Hogan's principles along with some alternative approaches that we have learned about the golf swing in the last few decades. That is why I have written this book.

# THE HANDS

Ben Hogan said, "good golf begins with a good grip." He believed and taught that a fundamentally correct grip allows the hands to work as a unit on the club—so important for consistent shotmaking. Hogan felt that golfers downplayed the value of a sound grip in terms of its contribution to speed, consistency and control of the clubhead through impact.

## Left Hand

Hogan favored a palm grip for the left hand, feeling that this offered the player a better chance for maintaining control of the club than if it were placed in the fingers. He said that the club should lie across the left hand so that it runs diagonally from the heel pad to the first joint of the index finger. Hogan also felt that pressure points in the grip were important for maintaining control. The main pressure points in the left hand were up from the last

Hogan placed the club well into the palm of the left hand.

Hogan felt that the club should not be placed down in the fingers of the left hand.

Grip pressure comes up from the last three fingers and down from the palm pad.

To maintain grip pressure is to maintain control.

**Left:** The V between thumb and forefinger of his left hand pointed to the right eye.

When grip pressure is lost, hands become loose and control is lost.

Hogan placed the club in the fingers of the right hand across the top joints.

three fingers and down from the fleshy palm-pad under the thumb. These pressure points helped prevent the club from coming loose during the swing, and helped keep the club solid at impact. When Hogan looked down at this completed left-hand grip, he saw that the V between his thumb and forefinger pointed toward his right eye.

### Right Hand

As opposed to the left hand, palm-oriented grip, Hogan believed that the club should be placed in the fingers of the right hand; specifically, the club should be placed across the top joints of the fingers—just below the palm. His thoughts about the right hand grip in general were that it should work equally with the left hand, but that it should not play an overpowering role in the swing.

To ensure that his hands worked as a unit, Hogan placed the little finger of his right hand in the groove between the index and second finger of his left hand. He then positioned the

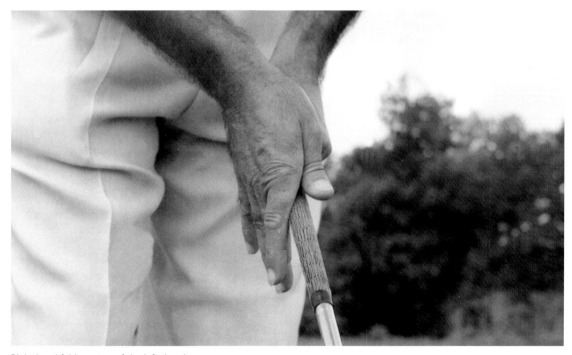

Right hand folds on top of the left thumb.

cavity in his formed right hand on top of his left thumb. Pressure in the right hand came from the middle two fingers and from the knuckle above the right index finger. When Hogan looked down at his completed right-hand grip, he saw that the V between his thumb and forefinger pointed to his chin (as opposed to the V in his left-hand grip pointing to his right eye). As a practice aid to neutralize the stronger right hand and also to feel how the hands should work together, Hogan practiced swinging the club (but not hitting a ball) with his right thumb and forefinger off the shaft.

Hogan wanted his grip to be secure, comfortable and alive, and tension free. A good grip allows the player to maintain control of the club and to hit the variety of shots—high and low shots, draws and fades—that are necessary if one is to become a complete player.

The little finger of the right hand fits in the groove between the first and second fingers of the left hand.

Left thumb fits in cavity of right hand.

The middle fingers supply the pressure.

15

Hogan suggests a drill in which you swing the club with the thumb and finger off the shaft.

Hogan had unusually flexible wrists and thumbs.

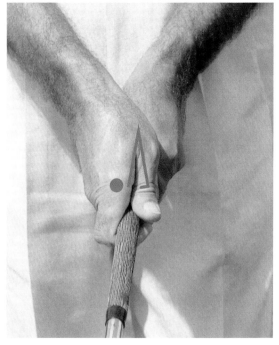

Hogan liked the V between thumb and forefinger of the right hand to point to the chin. The knuckle above the index finger helped provide pressure.

Checking grip pressure in the last three fingers of the left hand and middle two of the right.

Hogan advised golfers to work constantly on their grip to ensure it was perfect in every detail.

### My View

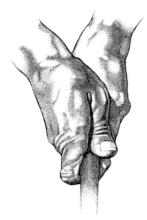

Hogan's grip looked immaculate. It was as if his hands were molded to the golf club. He wanted, as he indicated, a secure, alive, and comfortable grip—a grip that would offer the most effective means for him to control the ball. He never wanted his hands to come apart or separate from the club, so he worked long and hard at perfecting his grip, making a few changes to it over the years. The grip changes were an integral part of the much-discussed Hogan "secret." In his early years he had a severe problem with a wild hook, so naturally he built his swing around incorporating an anti-hook move. He was quoted as saying, "I hate a hook. It nauseates me. I could vomit when I see one." It's not surprising, then, that Hogan's "secret" was based on his finally being able to eliminate the hook from his game. I will discuss his "secret" in due course.

In my opinion most golfers run into big problems when they employ an ultra-palmy left-hand grip in the Hogan mode. You can see in

Club sits high in palm of Hogan's left hand.

the photograph of him taken down the line that the club sits extremely high in his palm. The problems are magnified when the palmy left-hand grip is combined with placing the club purely in the fingers of the right hand. Such a grip will, for most golfers, accentuate or even produce a slice; they will be unable to generate any real clubhead speed or to square the clubface in the impact area. Hogan, however, was able to master this method of gripping the club; in my opinion, not many players are able to handle it.

You see, Hogan was an exceptional athlete who had superb dynamics in his swing, meaning that he transferred collected energy to his clubhead in an astonishing, powerful fashion. He had strong, fast hands and his action was very much like cracking a bullwhip. His swing tempo was upbeat and he had tremendous overall flexibility, especially in the wrist/thumb area; the result was that he could swing the club back beyond parallel—far beyond parallel—at the top. Look at the curvature in his thumbs (see page 16); the way they bowed backward was extraordinary, and along with the flexibility in his wrists was a major part of the reason that he had so much wrist cock and clubhead lag in his swing. I first became aware of the flexibility in his thumb and wrist area after looking at still pictures of Hogan on his downswing when I was a kid, and I then tried to recreate the angles and the lag that he had coming down into the ball. That was considered a power position and I wanted to get into it. But I, along with just about every golfer I have encountered, had no chance of doing that. We don't have that flexibility in our wrist/thumb area.

So much flexibility and lag can also cause problems. A clubface even slightly closed when combined with tremendous lag and hand speed can lead to problems at impact, as it did at times for Hogan. With the longer clubs, especially the driver and fairway woods, and under the pressure of tournament play early in his career, a severe hook would show up. Hogan had to find a way to stop this shot and to pacify his hands so that he could gain more control.

Distance was never a problem, but control and timing were. Hogan thought that by changing his grip he would solve his directional problems—his strategy certainly went some way toward doing so.

Hogan made a couple of changes to his grip to cure his hook, and although he regarded these changes as minor, I feel they were major. He made the first change in 1945, when he shifted his left thumb up the shaft into what is considered a "short thumb" position. The "long thumb" (that is, where the thumb is stretched down the shaft as much as possible) encourages wrist cock, and so when Hogan shortened it he was able to firm up and restrict his wrist cock. This, in turn, had the effect of making his swing considerably shorter and keeping his club more under control at the top. By firming

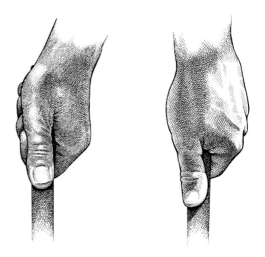

Short thumb          Long thumb

Short thumb—short swing.

Long thumb—long swing.

up his wrist cock he was also able to reduce the excessive amount of lag coming down. This greater control helped him improve his timing.

Having shortened the thumb up, Hogan's next step in his grip change was to move his left hand around in a counterclockwise direction (more to the left on the shaft), showing just one knuckle when he looked down on it; this placed his "short" left thumb over to the center as opposed to the right of the shaft. In conjunction with moving his left hand to the left he placed his right-hand grip more in his fingers and on top of the shaft, so that, I assume, each hand would match the other.

Consequently, his grip was now "weakened," to use a popular golfing term (though this does not mean it was weakened in strength). He felt the changes helped get the clubface more open; he could now hit hard with his right hand, without as much fear of the face closing and producing a hook. At the point of impact he could keep his left hand or lead hand firm and under control, and in turn have more control over the face. He had nearly achieved his goal of eliminating his hook. One more little key would solve the puzzle and eliminate the disastrous hooks that plagued him. That was his secret, which, as I have said, I will examine later.

Hogan felt that the changes he made were simply modifications to a sound grip and were particularly beneficial for him. It was no surprise, however, that many players copied Hogan's grip exactly, whether or not they had problems with hooking the ball. Many were unsuccessful in adopting his grip. Most golfers today, even tour players, can profitably adopt a slightly stronger grip with the hands (especially the left hand—showing two to three knuckles when you look down at it) turned in a more clockwise fashion to the right on the club; and they can do this without having to fear severe hooks. This is a more natural and advisable route to follow; it is more natural because your hands are in this position when they hang down by your side. Two players who employ ultra-strong grips—Paul Azinger and David Duval—are most assuredly controlled faders of the ball.

David Duval's strong left-hand grip.

There is more to curing a hook or promoting a fade than just weakening the grip.

Those of you who are thinking of shortening your left thumb to gain more control should bear in mind an important factor: namely, that Hogan's flexibility in his wrists and the curvature in his left thumb made it possible for him to shorten it on the club while still keeping the entire thumb flat on the grip. Most players by shortening the thumb would create a noticeable gap under the thumb, as it bunches up. This would lead to reduced rather than increased control of the clubhead because less of the thumb would be on the club. Generally, I prefer golfers to have a "longish" left thumb to aid cocking and leverage.

Hogan's grip looked great, no question. And it worked beautifully for him. The grip helped cure Hogan's hook. But most players don't hook the ball and in fact tend to slice the ball. Not only would the Hogan-like grip not cure their slice, it would make them hit some awfully big banana balls. A weak grip wouldn't be a cure. It would be a curse.

### To Become an 80-Breaker - or Better

I have tried to explain why Hogan gripped the club as he did. He obviously gave a lot of thought to the question of how to best come up with an anti-hook grip; so critical an element was this grip in his discussion of the fundamentals of golf that he devoted an entire chapter to it in *Five Lessons*. Gardner Dickinson, in fact, wrote that he thought the book "was, more than anything, a system of defense against a low, ducking hook, a problem that afflicts very few golfers." Hogan achieved the grip he wanted through trial and error, and his final version went a long way toward helping him develop tremendous control over his swing and the golf ball. At the same time there are alternatives to the manner in which he gripped the club. It is important to realize that Hogan's grip was a personal creation that helped him neutralize his tendencies. Art Wall, Jr., the 1959 Masters winner who played

frequently with Hogan, confirmed to me that Hogan, being such a fast swinger, used extremely heavy and stiff-shafted clubs—yet another obvious component of his anti-hook plan. (Hogan also used clubs with flat lies, another anti-hook measure.) His ability to control these clubs demonstrated how strong he was physically, and also how much clubhead speed he was able to create. Many players who tried to hit his clubs found that doing so was an exercise in futility. They simply could not handle such heavy, stiff clubs.

Hogan advocated a grip that positions the club in the palm of the left hand and purely in the fingers of the right hand. I share these ideas to a point, but I would advise some subtle changes especially for people who (1) do not have real suppleness in the wrists and thumbs, and (2) would like to hit a consistent draw—probably a large percentage of the world's golfers!

Let's first consider the left hand. In my experience, one of the most serious problems that golfers have is that they hold the club so much

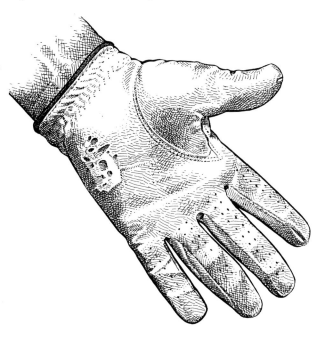

If the club sits too high in the palm, it's easy to wear a hole in the glove.

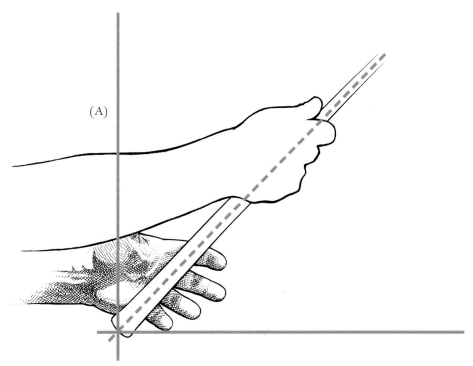

(A)

Positioning the club correctly in the left hand.

in the palm of the left hand that they tighten and freeze the wrist action. This makes it difficult for a golfer to cock the wrists correctly and to create any significant leverage. The club sits too high in the hand, to the extent that many golfers wear a hole in their gloves at the top of the palm. This is all brought about because the golfer feels a lack of power and tries to force some motion into the swing. The forced movement occurs mainly at the start of the swing, at the top of the backswing, and in the impact area. All this effort causes movement and friction between the hand and the grip of the club—the hole in the glove results. But a solution is available, a simple modification that for most people feels very good very quickly. It is quite amazing to see how easily the club works and the leverage that one creates when positioning the left hand properly; after all, the left hand acts as a hinge between the arm and the club, and promotes a fluid motion. The golfer feels that the club is in balance and

that little, if any, effort is required to produce power and "snap" in the swing. (I'll explain the solution in a moment.)

Hogan, because of his flexibility, had considerable natural leverage. His wrist action—the way he set the club going back and created so much snap with it through impact—helped him generate tremendous power. In an effort to create leverage and power, golfers need to correctly cock and uncock the wrists. If the golfer grips the club too much in the palm of his left hand then it is all too easy to lose leverage. A variety of common faults also arise, such as picking the club up from the start, rolling or fanning the clubface, the left arm breaking down, and the right elbow moving into a faulty position. The golfer compensates for, and reacts to, a bad grip by trying to force the club through, usually with the upper body, to try to generate some power. The wrist action of hitting a golf ball is rather like cracking a

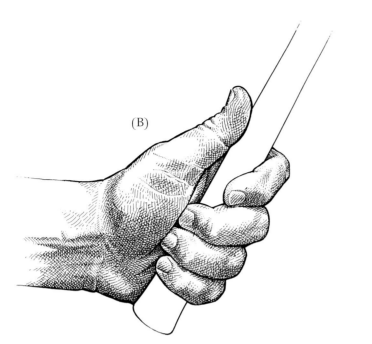

(B)

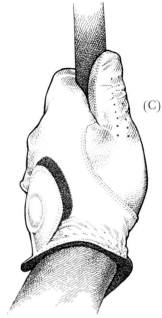

(C)

Neutral left hand grip: curve at base of wrist; two knuckles showing; V between thumb and finger points up toward your right ear.

Closing the left hand around the club.

whip; try to crack it with stiff, wooden wrists and see how the rest of the body incorrectly gets into the act to try to help. The problem of gripping the club too much in the palm of the left hand is so widespread that placing it correctly has frequently changed golfers overnight from being slicers into players who draw the ball, while turning short hitters into solid ball-strikers who now get some distance. That distance comes because the golfer is now able to cock his wrists correctly, create more snap and leverage, and really accelerate the club through the ball.

### Left Hand

Here's the way I'd like you to place your left hand on the club. Hold the club up in front of you in your right hand, angled at forty-five degrees to your body. Now bring your left hand from the target at ninety degrees to the shaft and place it on the club so that it fits diagonally across the palm (A) just under the base of the little finger running up through the crook of the forefinger (the midsection hinge where the forefinger bends). Now simply close your hand around the club (B). Let the thumb sit naturally as flush as possible straight down the shaft, neither overextending it nor shortening it, and place it close to the index finger. You should be able to see about two knuckles on your left hand (C) as you hold the club up in front of you; this is a "neutral" grip. (I'm sure Hogan, given his weak grip, would have seen only one knuckle if he held his hand up.) If you are a severe slicer try to see three knuckles—a "strong" grip. At the base of the wrist (the top of the glove) you should see a slight cup or curve. The V between the thumb and forefinger should point toward your right ear. This image will help you achieve a stronger grip. The left-hand grip is basically a palm grip, but the club is low down in the palm toward the fingers, which encourages movement and cocking in the wrist.

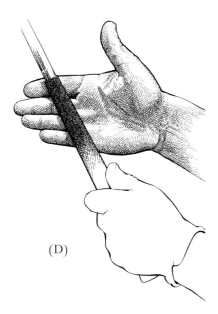

(D)

The right-hand grip is primarily a finger grip.

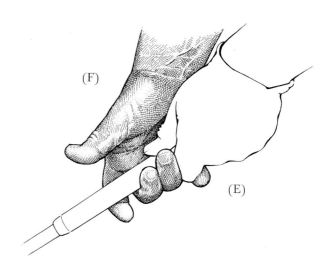

(F)

(E)

The right index finger and thumb form a "trigger" position

It is essential that you get this left-hand placement correct. Be precise with how you place your left hand on the club. Placing the club in your left hand in this manner should make you far more aware of the weight of the club without any tension in the hand. The wrist will now be in a favorable position to cock naturally and supply that all-important leverage. The final point regarding the left-hand grip is more of a preference than a fundamental, in that Hogan preferred to hold the club at the very end of the grip. I advise most players to hold the club so that about one-half to one inch is showing at the end beyond the little finger. Hogan felt that holding the club at the end allowed him to reduce some tension, and swing a touch slower. As I say, this is a matter of preference. Experiment to find what works best for you.

**Right Hand**
Now let's examine the right hand. Hogan liked the club to fit directly in the fingers, along the top joint line underneath the pad of the palm.

My contention is that if you held the club up with your right hand only, you would see that it would fit diagonally across your hand and in fact come into contact with the palm just below the little finger. I agree with Hogan's belief that the right-hand grip is basically a finger grip. But I feel that gripping the club diagonally across the right hand matches the diagonal look of the left hand. Most players, I believe, look more secure with this grip. Once again, hold the club up in front of you, this time with your left hand, at an angle of forty-five degrees. Place the club diagonally across the fingers of the right hand (D). Slide your hand down the club and link the baby finger between the first two knuckles of the left hand (E), a la Hogan. Now fold the right hand over the left thumb, so that the left thumb slots into the hollow underneath the thumb pad that the right hand provides in this position (F). It's important to neutralize the potentially destructive pincer action of the right index finger and thumb. Position the right index finger and thumb on the club in a trigger-like fashion while allowing a slight gap to form between

24

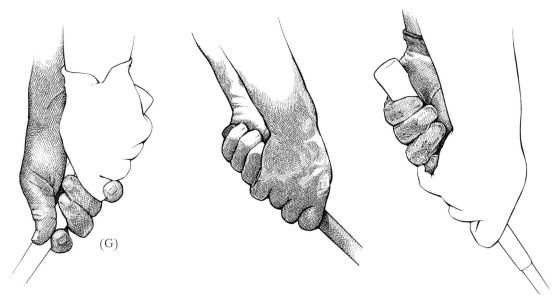

Hogan's preference was to hold the club at the top of the grip—I prefer players to have one-half to an inch showing.

the first two fingers (G). Without a trigger position, the tendency is for the right hand to grab the club like a hammer, which, apart from the extra tension, places the right arm and shoulder in too dominant a position at address.

**The key to getting a good grip every time (certainly while learning it) is to position the hands on the club while pointing it up in the air at forty-five degrees and looking at it at eye level. Most golfers have a poor grip because they attach their hands to the club while it is angled down to the ball, often grabbing it initially too high in the palm of the left hand and sloppily with the right hand. Trying to adjust your grip from this position is a losing battle. Why not get the grip right from the start? Be disciplined with the grip routine I've suggested and your grip will soon feel comfortable and natural.**

Because modern-day shafts taper to a large degree and many grips are very skinny at the lower end, I advise my students to add a couple of extra layers of tape under where the right hand fits. This thicker grip encourages a

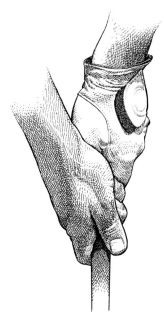

The end result of a disciplined approach— a correct and comfortable grip.

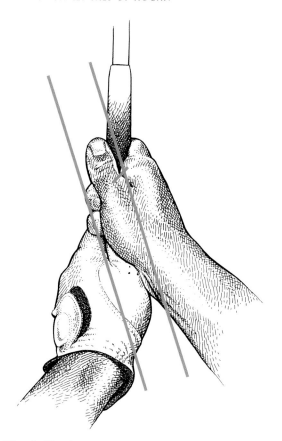

When looking down at your grip, your hands should generally be parallel to one another—with the V of the right hand pointed approximately toward the right shoulder.

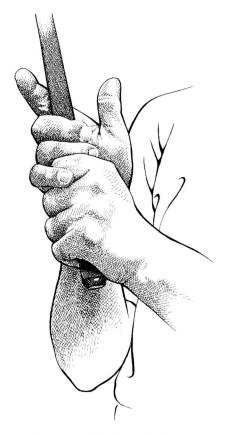

Hogan's modification to the Vardon grip.

more diagonal look and facilitates a trigger feeling rather than the hammer feeling. The V formed between the thumb and the forefinger on the right hand should point somewhere toward the right shoulder rather than toward the chin as Hogan suggested. However, if you are a good player who has problems hooking, I certainly would explore the idea of getting your right-hand grip a little more in the fingers and on top of the shaft, as Hogan did in order to promote a situation where you get the face more open at impact. It's one of those trial-and-error situations, and the weaker right hand might help. The general idea, then, is to encourage a grip where the hands are parallel to and match one another so that they sit uniformly on the club.

It is vital, as Hogan believed, that the hands work as a unit and not come apart. I've always

liked Hogan's slight modification to the Vardon grip—the idea of the baby finger of the right hand fitting between the index and second fingers rather than just riding piggyback as Vardon's did. Hogan's grip in my opinion joins the hands more solidly together and is the linking process I recommend. Although some great players with smaller hands do use an interlocking grip—Jack Nicklaus, Tom Kite, and Tiger Woods, to cite three—the overlapping or Vardon-type grip in my opinion puts less stress on the joints of the fingers and works better for players with medium-to-large size hands.

A few closing thoughts on the hands: in assuming your grip, do maintain pressure in the last three fingers of the left hand. Also place and maintain some pressure from the lifeline of the right hand onto the left thumb.

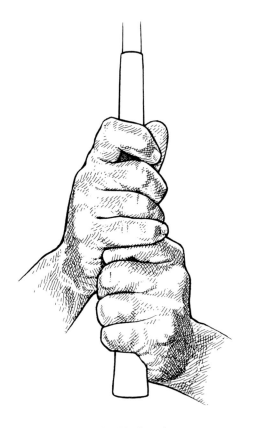

The original Vardon grip.

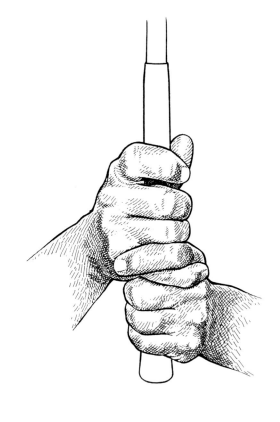

Interlocking grip.

This pressure will help keep the hands together and working in synch during the motion of the swing. The golfer who adopts the correct grip, where he feels the balance and weight of the swinging club without undue tension and is able to cock the wrists fully and freely, will usually feel comfortable with it immediately. Many people are wary of changing their grips because they are concerned that it will take them months to feel better with it. But I have found that the player willing to make the change will soon feel as if he has always held the club this way—in my view, the natural way. This grip works very well for all levels and ages of players—men and women, juniors and seniors, even tour players.

The grip I encourage my students to develop is still primarily a palm grip in the left hand and a finger grip in the right hand, but with some minor alterations that could make a world of difference to your game.

Finally, remember that a grip is not always as it appears. From the outside it may look quite good, but you can only assess a grip once you open it up and see how the club lies in the hands. Check your grip regularly because it's easy to revert to old habits. If you are going to transfer power through your hands into the clubhead, then you need to position your hands on the club perfectly every time. A good grip sends a strong message that you mean to play your best golf.

# ADDRESSING THE BALL

Ben Hogan felt that the address position was the next significant step after the grip. The "setup," as it is commonly called, consists of a golfer aligning himself properly to the target and then positioning his body in such a way that he can move freely during the swing while in balance. Setting up correctly, Hogan believed, would help accomplish the goal of creating power with the big muscles and then transferring it to the clubhead.

When Hogan moved into his setup, he aimed the clubface toward the target and then aligned his body to the clubface. His stance was fairly wide, giving a firm foundation for good balance. In Hogan's view, a golfer hitting a five-iron should place his feet about shoulder-width apart. The stance should be wider for longer

Right foot at ninety degrees, left foot turned out a quarter of a turn.

Hogan believed a splayed-out right foot can lead to swing problems.

clubs, and narrower for shorter ones. A stance that is too wide or too narrow will compromise balance and freedom of motion.

Hogan proposed that the golfer place his right foot at ninety degrees to the target line and then place his left foot into position about a quarter of a turn toward the target—approximately twenty degrees. A golfer who sets his left foot in this manner would not over-rotate his hips as he swung the club back. However, Hogan felt that splaying out the right foot in the same manner and not ninety degrees to the target would promote swaying, dipping or collapsing the left arm because of the excessive freedom which the turned-out right foot

provides. These faults lead to a weak, uncoiled position at the top of the backswing. Pointing the right foot out can also force the arms and club to move out and around the right hip as they make their way down to the ball.

No less esteemed an observer of the swing than two-time U.S. Open champion and Masters winner, Cary Middlecoff, believed that Hogan's advice to turn the left foot outward had long been standard procedure. "That goes at least back to (Harry) Vardon," Middlecoff wrote, "and it has always been generally agreed that this positioning of the left foot facilitates the downswing movement of the hips and makes it easier for the player to move freely through the ball."

In thinking about the arms at address, Hogan agreed with the long-held principle that the player should strive to achieve a maximum arc. Horace Hutchinson, the 1886 and 1887 British Amateur champion, and a respected author, wrote in 1895 that, "In leaving the ball, the clubhead should swing back as far as possible," and that the arms should be allowed "to go to their full length as the clubhead swings away from the ball, or as nearly to their full length as is possible without further stretching." Nearly half a century later, Bobby Jones wrote that the arc of the swing should be "made very broad so that space and time for adding speed to the clubhead coming down will be as great as possible." Hogan was certainly following accepted theory in advocating a maximum arc. Hogan worked on the premise that at least one arm needs to be straight or fully extended throughout the swing—a key to achieving a maximum arc, power and consistency.

Inner elbows pointing to the sky: Hogan's image of a rope binding the arms.

At address, Hogan wrote that the upper parts of the arms pressed against the chest and the elbows were close together and pointing toward their corresponding hipbone. He pointed out that the pocket of each elbow—the small depression on the inside of the joint—should face the sky and not its opposite. His image at address was of a rope binding the elbows and arms together. He wanted the golfer to maintain that elbows/arms relationship throughout the swing. And while he spoke about the left arm hanging straight at address, he advised that the right arm should have a slight bend at the elbow. This allows the right elbow to fold close to the body as the club is swung back and to point to the ground (the ideal position in his opinion) at the top of the backswing.

Hogan's final point regarding the address position concerned posture—the way a golfer positions his trunk and knees. His mental image was of a golfer starting with an erect position at address, and then sitting down a couple of inches as if sitting on a seat stick (see page 33). This semi-sitting position would give the player a sense of heaviness in the buttocks

Elbows should not face each other.

THE FUNDAMENTALS OF HOGAN

Left arm hanging straight.

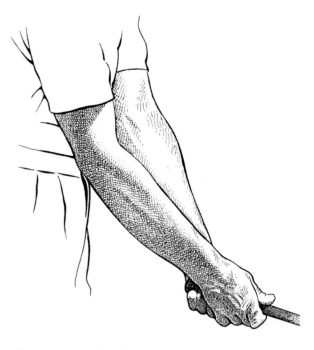

Left arm hangs straight, right arm kinked in.

Hogan exaggerating excessive knee flex.

Hogan mimicking poor posture.

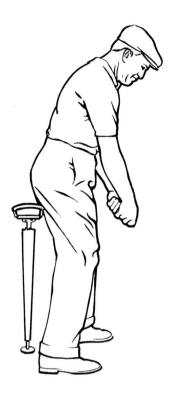

To practice posture, start by standing erect and setting the clubhead above the ball.

and promote liveliness in the lower legs, and, in Hogan's view, put the weight back towards the heels. There must be no slouching of the shoulders, stiffness in the legs, or collapsing of the knees, as seen in many golfers. Tommy Armour, the superb teacher and player who won the 1927 U.S. Open, the 1930 PGA Championship and the 1931 British Open, recommended a similar position. As he wrote, "You will stand as upright as you can to the ball; not stiff, but comfortably upright with the knees flexed a little bit." Hogan also advocated a flexed knee position and in addition liked the knees to be pinched slightly inward (the right knee a fraction more than the left). By placing himself in this very athletic position, Hogan felt he was completely stabilized and balanced at address, ready to make the proper swing.

**My View**

Still pictures cannot possibly capture the athleticism of Hogan's setup. His setup was powerful, alive, ready for action, and very purposeful. His tall posture with very little forward

Complete your posture by lowering yourself and placing the clubhead behind the ball.

When taking his actual address, Hogan's foot was not as square as he suggested.

upper-body bend or knee flex was determined by his build—just under 5 feet 9 inches tall with long arms and strong gluteus maximus muscles; his rear end, to put it delicately, was sizable and strong. This encouraged him to stand erect and—in his case—facilitated his shoulders turning on a flat horizontal plane, which produced the flattish, characteristically Hoganesque swing plane. Hogan said he liked to feel his weight back on his heels. But I sense that his balance was more forward, toward the arches and the balls of his feet, as is the case with most athletes—for example, in basketball, where the shooter sets himself for a free throw. Photographs of Hogan suggest that even though he stood tall, his weight was not back on his heels as much as he thought.

Hogan's address provided a firm base, while his wide stance contributed greatly to his immaculate balance throughout his swing. One has to remember that Hogan's suppleness and range of motion were something to behold. It is not surprising that he had to rein himself in to some degree, so that he would not stretch and turn as much as his flexibility allowed. Only in this manner could he keep his swing under control. One of these restrictors or governors, which Hogan always emphasized and used to curtail his hip turn on his backswing, was having his right foot fairly square as opposed to turned out. I say "fairly square" because although he states his right foot is ninety degrees to the target, he does seem to turn the foot out a little in nearly all of the photographs I have viewed of him at address. I find that many players—especially those lacking in suppleness—who adopt a perfectly square right foot, struggle to make a turn on the backswing; as a result they cut their shoulder and hip turns short. As far as the left foot goes, I agree with Hogan that the ideal approach is to turn it out at approximately twenty degrees. Having measured how far Hogan turns his left foot out, I was intrigued to learn that it was at least thirty degrees. In any case, I might suggest that a player who has a problem with an exaggerated lateral hip slide (where the hips move well forward toward the target before they turn to the left) turn the left foot out less than twenty degrees to help offset the problem.

It's worth noting the adjustments Hogan made in his address position which were directly related to his desire not to hook the ball. I have referred to his weak left-hand grip and the way he placed the club in the fingers of his right hand. The result was that his right arm was positioned at address well above his left arm—an anti-hook position if ever I saw one. As far as the rest of his alignment is concerned, Hogan did not have a conventionally square setup, in which the body lines—feet, knees, hips, and shoulders—are set parallel to the target line. His clubface looked to the target but his feet were closed—aimed right—and his knees, hips, and shoulders were slightly open—aimed left of his intended target.

It's also worth pointing out that with his irons and his woods Hogan had his hands in the center of his stance, almost giving the impression that they were behind the ball. This calls to mind the way turn-of-the-century players set up to the ball. Most players, certainly the modern tour players, place their hands ahead of the ball. My preference is to have them slightly behind the ball with the driver, to encourage a more upward swing that will sweep the ball off the tee; and with the irons, to have the hands slightly further forward to encourage a descending, squeezing blow onto the ball.

Hogan, in keeping with his theme of allowing no wasted motion in his swing, provides the image in which his arms are bound together, his intent being to demonstrate the importance of keeping the elbows and arms as close together as possible during the swing. I don't think this helps most players. The image suggests, to some extent, tightness and tension at address, rather than the togetherness that Hogan sought. However, if you study the way Hogan actually positioned his arms at address,

Anti-hook setup: right arm above left.

In reality, Hogan's arms looked relaxed, and not bound tightly together, as he advised.

they really did not appear tight; in fact, quite the opposite. They look fairly soft, as he advised they should be. (Hogan wrote, "This is a very pleasant game and unnatural straining is not at all necessary or desirable.") Also, he did not at address have the inner part of each elbow—the "pocket"—looking at the sky as much as he suggested; his elbows looked somewhere in between a bowed-out position and the location he recommends. Hogan obviously felt more secure with an image of keeping his arms close together and tight to his chest at the start. If he wanted a feeling of connectedness—a sense of feeling tight and compact throughout the swing—then, he reasoned, why not begin that way? Much of his arm location was intentionally designed to get his right elbow in tight and close to the body at the top of the swing. This may have been ideal for his level of flexibility, but would not, I feel, suit the vast majority of golfers. More on this point later.

Hogan makes an excellent suggestion in advising golfers to adopt an athletic semi-sitting position at address rather than the sloppy setup many players use. However, keep in mind that while Hogan's setup appeared wonderfully athletic and poised, there remains the fact that one's build plays an important factor in constructing a solid posture and stance. It certainly did in Hogan's case. Not every golfer can conform to an ideal model. Whether you are short or tall, flexible or inflexible, have short legs or short arms, long legs or long arms, whether you are stout or slim—all these factors enter into the setup equation. As a result, every player will look different at address. The key at address is that you should be stable and balanced, and develop a feeling of maintaining this balance throughout your swing. You want to be able to move freely at speed, as Hogan did, and as he proved by his great length and phenomenal accuracy. His posture looked dynamic, but relaxed. You can develop just as effective and consistent a setup as Hogan did; however, you will look very different than he did.

## To Become an 80-Breaker—or Better

Great players all have their own distinctive looks when standing to the ball. Simply, their different stances and postures are largely determined by their different body types. The common denominator in all exemplary setups is that they allow the golfer to put himself in an athletic "ready" position from which to move a stationary club and build it up to exceptional speed. This requires impeccable balance. Building a firm foundation is vital to this task.

We are really looking for an athletic setup to prepare for the action that will follow. Generally speaking, I agree with Hogan that the upper body should be fairly erect, as this definitely counteracts the tendency many golfers have to get slouchy, hunched and bent over at address, which seriously limits a good body motion. On the other hand, some players who think tall (or erect) at address might set the upper body too vertically with the head and neck held too high in a tense position. This can result in an address where there is hardly any forward tilt of the torso; this military look is no good either. Hogan's build basically determined his "tall" look, and he appeared very comfortable standing this way. There were approximately twenty degrees of forward bend in his upper body when he was using a driver, whereas most players probably average around the thirty-degree mark. It is interesting to note that Hogan's upper body did in fact tilt more forward early in his career, which probably accounted for his more upright swing plane then.

The forward bend or "spine angle"—the term often used—determines the angle on which the shoulders turn and rotate. The thirty-degree bend will allow the shoulders to turn on a slightly steeper, more tilted axis than will the twenty-degree bend. This will facilitate the arms swinging on a more upright plane compared to Hogan's flat shoulder and arm plane. I usually prefer a freer, more upright plane so I'm in favor of most players adopting approximately a thirty-degree forward bend. The taller

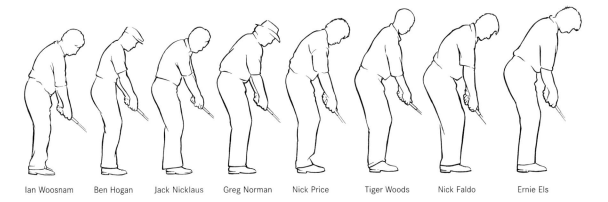

| Ian Woosnam | Ben Hogan | Jack Nicklaus | Greg Norman | Nick Price | Tiger Woods | Nick Faldo | Ernie Els |

All great players look different standing to the ball; posture is determined by body type. The common denominator is that each player is in an athletic, "ready" position.

posture that Hogan adopted in mid-career certainly was a factor in his swinging on a flatter plane. I know this sounds contrary to what you might think, because common sense would suggest that if you stand upright then you will swing upright. This might be the case were a golfer simply to lift his arms to make his backswing. But if you turn correctly—and we will discuss how to do this—an upright posture normally produces a more horizontal shoulder turn, which results in a flatter plane. The reverse is obviously true for a stance that is more bent over, which results in a more vertical shoulder turn and a more upright swing plane.

The key to good posture, I keep emphasizing to players, is to have a straight lower back and a relaxed, slightly rounded upper-body and neck, whereby the arms can just hang. Too straight an upper body with the shoulders held back will produce undue tension. Focusing on a straight lower back helps stabilize the lower body and encourages the trunk and spine to rotate back and through on a consistent axis. It is essential, then, to set the spine at the proper angle—that is, to have the correct amount of forward bend from the hips in conjunction with the right amount of knee flex.

In order for the address position to be athletic, spine angle and knee flex will vary somewhat from player to player depending on their builds (that is, the length of a player's back, legs, and arms). The club a player is using also influences the degree of forward bend; there will be more forward bend when a player is using a wedge than a three-iron. Overall, the important concept to grasp is that whatever angles you create at address, you should maintain them throughout your swing, certainly up until impact, anyway. Hogan maintained his angles exceptionally well.

There is an obvious sense in which the golf swing could be considered a geometrical motion. It comprises various arcs, planes, lines, and angles. It helps to understand some of these elements, particularly at address, and to keep a picture of them in your mind's eye. This is of enormous help in developing a powerful, repetitive swing. In my opinion, the most important element for a golfer to be aware of is the angular position he places his body in at address. You could simply say this: adopting a good posture will in itself go a long way toward ensuring that your swing is geometrically sound.

Hogan advocates that the golfer place his feet shoulder-width apart for a normal five-iron shot. I maintain that for a person with an average build this shoulder width should be the maximum, and that it should apply to a driver, not a five-iron. This same player should place his feet less than shoulder-width apart for the other clubs—progressively narrower from the long irons through the short irons. Here again, Hogan's advice may be entirely appropriate for a tall person with long legs who needs to improve his balance, or for a good player whose legs are overactive during the swing. My reasoning for suggesting a narrower stance than Hogan advocates is this: many players who don't have the athletic ability to move at speed, in balance, need to focus on a freer movement with the arms and hands and to limit excessive body motion. Too wide a stance can easily encourage body motion in the form of swaying back or lunging forward. A narrower stance encourages a freer hand and arm swing and helps promote good rhythm. It also helps you establish a nice flow with the club. **I even suggest an exercise at times in which players hit balls with their feet six inches apart to promote this action. Try this if you feel you are all body and lack power.**

I used the word "excessive" in the previous paragraph. By excessive I mean wasted, and we don't want wasted motion in the swing. Although it obviously did not affect Hogan adversely, it is interesting to note that with the driver he slid his right foot toward the target prior to impact quite appreciably at times. This indicated that his stance was very wide, but obviously he deemed it necessary in order to develop the leverage to hit his driver hard. And he certainly did hit his driver hard.

In my teaching I've observed that players who are overly wide at address tend to overuse the body in a way that reduces clubhead speed and results in the clubface not striking the ball squarely. This inordinate amount of body motion leads to a weak hit at the ball; and, of course, it is at impact where the player learns the effect of what has gone before in his swing, as the quality of the shot is expressed. Get things right before impact and you have a much better chance of getting them right at impact.

I feel the distance between the insteps of the feet should be the same as the width of the shoulders for the driver, and progressively narrower as the club gets shorter.

**Drills, as always, help a player develop the right positions. I am going to suggest one in which you do not use a club; I like my students to work on this in the interest of building up an athletic posture. First, set your feet a comfortable distance apart; again, slightly narrower than Hogan suggests. Having positioned your feet comfortably, place your hands on your hips. Stand straight up and look out in front of you. Flex your knees a touch and now simply roll your hips forward so that your tailbone moves out and up—your lower back will feel straight. Sense that you are bending from the hips and not from the waist; you should be in a position now that enables you to rock quite easily from your toes to your heels. This means that your weight is now**

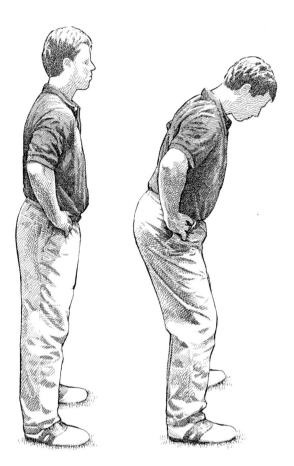

Developing an athletic posture.

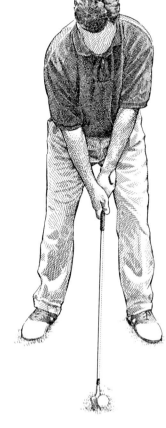

Both feet turned out about twenty degrees.

through the center of your feet and is directly supporting your mass. Practice this at home in front of a mirror without your shoes on to better sense the balance you have created. You also need to sense the firmness and resistance of the ground—the floor in this case—when working on your setup. It's a wonderful feeling that provides the swing with a solid foundation. When you move from this position to take a club in your hands, you will find that moving your arms in front of you automatically rounds your shoulders and upper body into a relaxed position—not slouched but athletically poised.

Most people would benefit from turning the right foot out slightly. Turn it out unless you

have so much flexibility that you need to inhibit your hip turn on the backswing, as Hogan did. But you are probably not as elastic as he was. The rule is that if you require more motion to complete your turn, then turn the right foot out; if you require less, turn it in. Experiment to find what suits you best. My preference is that on average I like to see both feet turned out about twenty degrees. This promotes a good turn in both directions.

Now let's focus on the location of the arms. Continuing on from the posture drill where you aren't using a club, just clap your hands to get your arms relaxed and in the position where the elbows look approximately at the hips.

Clapping hands puts the arms in the ideal relaxed position.

Right arm below left promotes a draw.

This clapping movement puts your arms in a tension-free and "soft" position and will give you the Hogan look once you slide the right hand below the left. When I'm looking down the line at a person addressing the ball, I prefer to see the arms positioned parallel to the target line (not with the right arm above the left, a position Hogan appears to exaggerate), unless the golfer is intending to fade the ball. In fact, as Hogan is showing here without a club, it is far preferable to have the right arm set lower than the left if you want to draw the ball.

I do like the way Hogan pulls his right foot back when using the longer clubs so that he appears slightly closed (aimed right) relative to the target line, where his feet are concerned. This line across the toes gives a player a clear

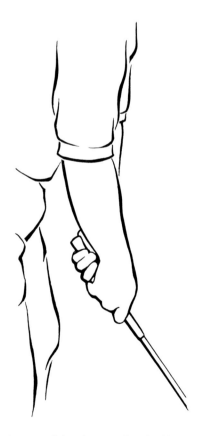

Arms parallel to the target line at address.

Right foot pulled back in closed position; eyes, shoulders, hips, knees parallel to target line.

Left hip set higher at address, right knee kicked in.

image on the downswing of the preferred inside path back to the ball. Pulling the right foot back also provides another benefit. It encourages not only the proper path for the swing, but also promotes the right side getting out of the way on the backswing almost in symmetry with the right foot being turned out (a considerable help to those senior golfers who lack flexibility). I would, however, advise you when working on aim and alignment to get the rest of your body—knees, hips, shoulders, and eye line—as parallel as possible to the target line.

Some final points: I love the way Hogan appears at address from behind. Note how his left hip is set higher and his right knee is kicked in slightly. This helps place the spine in a slightly tilted position away from and behind the ver-

tical. And certainly with the woods this gives the golfer a clear image of getting behind the ball on the backswing, and staying behind it through impact. It is helpful to place the right knee in a little, and to set the left hip approximately an inch higher than the right hip; this position will automatically set the right side a little lower.

To further elaborate on the knees, I agree with having the right knee pinched in a bit, but I'm not a fan of pointing the left knee in. Generally, this inward look with both knees inhibits the turn and can actually encourage a reverse pivot. I advise golfers to set the left knee on top of the inside of the left foot. I think it looks and feels more natural.

I've written briefly in the middle section of this chapter about Hogan's tallish, erect address. As I have explained, I like as a rule to see more forward bend with the upper body than Hogan had. But as with all things in golf, there is a certain amount of leeway. For instance, if a student tilts his shoulders on too steep of a plane on the backswing and as a result swings the club very upright, I will suggest that he consider Hogan's taller posture and subsequent flatter shoulder rotation. If on the backswing a golfer turns his shoulders on too flat a plane and there's a distinct lack of coiling and stretching, I may get him to bend forward more, thereby encouraging more shoulder tilt to increase the coil.

Remember that the setup (along with the grip, of course) is a constant in the swing, an element you should be able to repeat and control because it is a static position. There's no reason you should be unable to get it right, especially if you work with a mirror. I work harder with players—especially tour players—on the setup than on any other area. *Players constantly change their setups without realizing they have done so.* This is understandable because it's difficult to put yourself into a golfing address position every day. Twisting, bending, tilting: these are not natural positions for anybody. And add to this the fact that one day you might be playing a very hilly course where you have uneven lies, and the next day you might be playing in strong winds or in extremely wet conditions where you're trying to get a wider stance to secure your feet. There are all sorts of reasons why your setup might change. You might have a little fatigue. Ernie Els is a prime example. Toward the end of the season he gets tired and his address tends to become saggy. He starts to get noticeably lower in his posture, and as a result his backswing begins to get a little cramped and he makes compensations on his downswing. And

it all starts with his posture. It's very important to check your posture constantly because it will change without your even being aware of it, and as a result your swing will change.

*Bad posture is the root cause of many problems that occur during the swing. Be disciplined and examine your posture at every opportunity. It's important to recognize what good posture means in golf, and the only way to do this is to monitor it. You will be rewarded for your efforts and patience. Believe me when I say that stance and posture are absolutely basic to an improved swing. It's true for the best golfers. It's true for every golfer.*

I would also like to write briefly about club fitting. It is important to get clubs that fit you so that you can perfect your setup and build a repeating swing. For example, a short person who plays with a standard lie may well feel that the toe of the club sits off the ground—too upright of a lie and one that tends to create shots that go left: this person needs flatter clubs. A tall person using a standard lie club could find the heel sitting off the ground—too flat of a lie and one that tends to create shots that go right: this person needs more upright clubs. The sole of the club should sit relatively flush on the turf. Otherwise, through no fault of your own, you'll make compensations in your swing in order to hit the ball straight. These compensations will inevitably groove errors into your swing. It is advisable to be professionally fitted with clubs, not only to get the lie and length right, but also for shaft flex, material (for example, graphite or steel), weight, grip thickness, and head design—each plays a role in controlling direction and maximizing distance. If you buy a set of clubs from an experienced club-fitter to suit you and your swing, you will have increased your chances of playing to your potential. Good technique and correctly-fitted clubs go hand in hand.

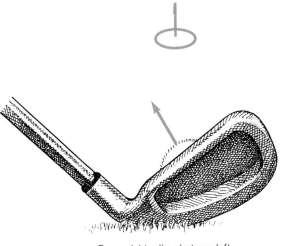

Too upright a lie, shots go left.

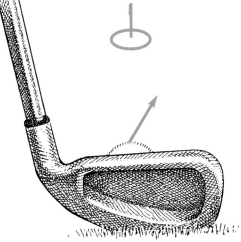

Too flat a lie, shots go right.

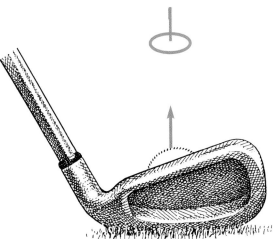

Correct lie, shots on line.

# THE BACKSWING

By 1946, having studied the golf swing for years and even, occasionally, having taught it, Ben Hogan felt he understood its dynamics. He had worked with purpose, determination and for long hours on his own, and had also been open-minded enough to learn from other people. For instance, fellow touring pro Ky Laffoon offered Hogan some advice on driving on the practice tee at the Tacoma Country Club during a tournament. Hogan was a sponge-always studying, always experimenting, always refining, and always learning. In fact, he dedicated his first book, *Power Golf*, to Henry Picard, an outstanding player and teacher of his time. Picard helped Hogan periodically with his game and was instrumental in Hogan modifying his grip to stop hooking the ball.

The waggle should emulate the path and speed of the backswing.

During the waggle the right elbow touches the front of the right hip; the left elbow rotates a little.

The proof of Hogan's hard-earned knowledge was on display in the big championships. In 1946 he won the PGA Championship and twelve other tournaments, and finished the season as the tour's leading money-winner. Hogan had proven to himself that his swing stood up under the most severe pressure, which was the test it was designed to meet. He felt confident in his swing because he had developed a method that, for him, was all but impregnable.

Not surprisingly, given Hogan's attention to detail, he felt that every aspect of the swing was important. To Hogan, there was nothing frivolous about any aspect to the swing, or the preparation to swing. This was noticeable to the finest degree in the emphasis he placed upon the waggle. He felt that the waggle was instrumental in helping the golfer make the transition from setting up the ball to starting the backswing. Hogan studied the waggle with all the attention a scholar would devote to a research problem and its solution. It was meant to help the golfer gain a sense of the shot and a feel for the upcoming swing. The waggle, a form of mini-swing, prepared the golfer for the rhythm and feel that the upcoming full swing demanded.

"Hogan", wrote Cary Middlecoff, "placed more emphasis on the waggle than any swing theorist before." He pointed out that Hogan himself had first become aware in 1932 of how crucial the waggle was when he observed the advantage that Johnny Revolta gained by using it for short shots around the green. Hogan elaborated on this idea and applied it to his complete game.

While Hogan's waggle was uniquely his own, he also thought that it should vary depending on the type of shot to be played. A high, soft shot might call for a slow waggle. An aggressive, low shot into the wind might require a quicker, snappier waggle. Yet, even though Hogan believed that the waggle should emulate the path and speed of the backswing, he knew that it was different in one major area—in the waggle, the shoulders are not involved, whereas in the swing they are. This relates to Hogan's feeling that the swing is a chain reaction. During the backswing, the hands moved first, followed by the arms, shoulder and lower body. The order was then reversed on the downswing—lower body, shoulders, arms and hands. This sequence was critical, according to Hogan, and the golfer who accomplished it could strike a ball with tremendous force.

Once the proper sequence is in motion on the backswing, it pulls the hips around and the left knee turns inward just about the time the hands approach hip height. The shoulders, meantime, should rotate as far as possible around a rock-solid head. Regarding this rock-solid head, it's interesting to consider a letter that Hogan wrote to a fellow who watched him play an exhibition match in Fort Worth. "The center of gravity of the body must stay in one place throughout the swing," Hogan counseled. "That is, if a line is drawn through the nose or head to the ground, the head must stay in that position throughout the swing." Hogan had also referred to the stationary head in *Power Golf*. "Your head doesn't move," he declared. Most golfers, Hogan pointed out, don't complete the turn because they finish the backswing (falsely) by bending the left arm and weakly lifting the club to the top, thereby losing power. A checkpoint for a proper, true shoulder turn is that the left shoulder should touch the chin at the top of the backswing.

Hogan also had a theory about the hips. The idea is to create resistance in the hips as the shoulders wind up, which maximizes a player's "coil". Any early turning of the hips on the backswing would destroy this coil. During the backswing, the goal is to create a stretching feeling in the muscles between the hips and shoulders. This stretch will make the downswing a fairly instinctive reaction to what has gone before, and it is a movement that is led by the hips as they start to turn

At the top of the backswing the chin should contact the top of the left shoulder.

Left knee breaks in toward the right.     Hogan checks the stability of his right knee by placing a club next to his leg.

Hogan describes the backswing plane as an inclined angle running up from the ball through the shoulders.

If the club is on plane, it is easier for the upper body to link up with the lower body when the arms swing down.

Ben Hogan's image of his swing plane.

back. The continuation of the chain reaction adds further torsion to the muscles, thereby allowing the shoulders, arms and hands to unwind quickly back to the ball, creating impressive clubhead speed.

Also during the backswing, as mentioned, the left knee moves a bit to the right. The left foot, as well, rolls slightly inward. Proper footwork has been a cornerstone of swing theory down the years. Hogan did feel, however, that it was important not to exaggerate the footwork. He felt that the left heel should never lift more than an inch off the ground. If it does, balance will be sacrificed. To prevent swaying, Hogan believed that the right leg should stay in the same position it was in at address. His way of checking this during practice was to place a club to the outside of his right leg at address and make sure it remained at precisely the same angle as he moved to the top of his backswing.

When speaking about the shape of the swing and the motion of the arms, Hogan explained it in terms of the "plane" of the swing. He said there were two planes: a backswing plane and a downswing plane. This was quite a departure from the accepted theory that the swing was essentially circular and traveled up and down on the same path. He first mentioned this idea of two planes in *Power Golf*. Hogan wrote that on the downswing the club travels "inside of the arc it described going back on the backswing."

Hogan viewed the backswing plane as an inclined angle taken at address, running up through the shoulders from the ball. With the left forearm acting as guide for the whole motion, the shoulders, arms, hands and club should rotate on this plane and not deviate from it. By following this imaginary track, the upper body and arms will be in a position at the top of the swing that allows them to come down in concert with the lower body, thereby maximizing power and accuracy without any wasted motion.

He believed that if a person could get a picture in his mind's eye of the plane he would be far more likely to produce a repeating motion. The visual image that worked for Hogan was a large, tilted pane of glass extending up from the ball and resting on the golfer's shoulders while he is in his address position, with his head poking through a hole in the glass. To achieve a correct backswing, the golfer needed to ensure that his arms were parallel to the glass (the plane) not only as they approached hip level but all the way to the top. The arms would attain this position if the shoulders turned on the same angle as the glass. Once at the top, the left arm must still be parallel to the pane. It was okay if the backswing were a bit flatter than the correct plane but not if it were upright and above, thereby shattering the imaginary pane of glass. Swinging above the correct plane also forced players to make adjustments to avoid the imaginary glass on the way down; i.e., a player either swinging way outside of it or having to reroute the club back behind the pane in order to find a proper path down to the ball. These compensations lead to mis-hit shots and overall inconsistency. Once Hogan understood how to swing to the top of his backswing on what he felt was his optimum plane, he solved his problems of inconsistency. By learning to repeat and groove this motion through hitting thousands of balls and spending countless hours in front of a mirror, he was able to build total confidence in his swing and his ability to control the golf ball.  The result of all this work was that Hogan consistently shot lower scores.

**My View**

Hogan's conviction that the proper setup and address provide the proper foundation for the backswing, and that the backswing then sets up the downswing, is sound. One cannot go wrong in following this idea, which was so typical of Hogan's meticulous thinking.

In his lifelong quest for golfing perfection, Hogan delved into one of golf's abiding challenges. The challenge is that golf is about hitting a stationary ball; you must find a way to put yourself into motion, given that there is no exter-

nal stimulus to motivate you to start the swing. It's not like baseball, for instance, where the batter reacts to a pitch, or tennis, where the person receiving the serve reacts to the ball. In golf the stationary ball can create confusion as a player gets ready to hit, so much so that his thinking can become destructive and ruin any chance of making a good swing.

That's why a bridge is needed from setting up to the ball to starting the swing. Hogan, through study and practice, answered the challenge of the stationary ball by finding that bridge. His answer was the waggle.

I really like the way Hogan places so much emphasis on the waggle—most golfers don't attach enough importance to it. He was very purposeful with his waggle; it played a crucial role in his developing and maintaining a repeating swing. His waggle was basically a mini-version of his full swing where he tried to get the face open; it was very much the waggle of a player who tried to rotate the clubface open in the backswing. At the same time, a waggle ought to play a part in every golfer's game.

Amateurs, and sometimes even professionals, tend to think themselves into a frenzy to the point that they sometimes tighten up and even freeze at address; often they have too many swing thoughts or they harbor disastrous images of poor shots. They thereby lose the all-important sequencing rhythm and flow to start the swing. Most problems in the swing, after all, begin with either a faulty address or from the starting move. The waggle is important in that it adds motion and rhythm to a static address position and promotes a repetitive start to the swing; it also aids in releasing tension. In essence, it helps generate a productive rather than a destructive golfing mind during this important time period.

But even a productive golfing mind will not compensate for a poor swing. Solid golf shots result from swings that are dynamically sound. Hogan was obviously very aware of the

Hogan focusing on tucking his right elbow.

Hogan's backswing in the early years involved an active lower body and high hands.

biomechanics of the swing, whether consciously or intuitively. He was keenly aware of the way the various parts—hands, arms, shoulders, and hips—had to move in sequence in the swing to produce energy and power. In developing this power one has to create torque by turning, stretching, and coiling on the backswing and then releasing this stored-up energy on the downswing. Hogan's flexibility enabled him to do all this while keeping his head almost dead still during the swing, which is difficult for most golfers. He was able to create enormous torque by turning his shoulders fully while resisting with his hips, and he did so while swinging on a fairly flat plane with a tucked right elbow. Golfers who don't have Hogan's suppleness or range of motion would not, in my opinion, develop the necessary torque required to hit solid, on-line shots if they were to work on keeping their heads dead still, tucking their right elbow, and swinging on so flat a plane. There's no question about it: Hogan's swing suited his build, his flexibility, and his

Hogan's swing evolved into the look with which he was always associated—a flat plane.

Hogan had a long swing during the first part of his career.

Hogan's swing became shorter and more compact.

own particular movement patterns. Other players trying to copy his moves would probably get tied up in knots.

In his early years, Hogan had an extremely long backswing (especially with the woods), a very big hip turn in conjunction with an active left foot and knee, and a colossal shoulder turn accompanied by fairly high hands—he was definitely more upright in those days. His extreme flexibility and suppleness enabled him to make this swing quite easily. After Hogan came out of the army at the end of the war he worked very hard on improving his technique. His primary goal was to eliminate the disastrous hook that very early in his career kept him from winning. Although he played a lot of great golf prior to his accident in 1949, Hogan was still worried about the hook that appeared periodically and cost him some tournaments.

Incredibly, despite his near-fatal car accident

in 1949, Hogan was able to produce his best golf following his recovery. He won six of his nine majors between 1950 and 1953. It is still amazing to realize that in 1953 he won the Masters, the U.S. Open, and the British Open. Hogan could not play the PGA Championship (then a match play event) because it was held the week prior to the British Open; the final match, in fact, was played the day before the British Open began. It was impossible, due to the scheduling, for any golfer to even contemplate winning the Grand Slam of all four majors in 1953, let alone actually win them.

In studying Hogan's swing, I feel that after World War II ended in 1945 and until the early 1950s it went through a series of changes, not the least of which was that his backswing became shorter and more compact. This occurred for a variety of reasons: he incorporated some technical swing changes, along with a change to his grip, to cure his hook; his

Hogan's reverse pivot!

Jose Maria Olazabal: one of a number of top players who "hang" on their left side—the lower body leaning toward the target.

car accident; and possibly the fact that he was getting a little older. These changes improved his swing, which now had fewer sources of error, and so started to lead to the reliability, consistency, and control that he sought with passion and commitment.

Hogan's swing after his accident took on the look with which he will always be associated—a flat swing plane. He was the first well-known player of his era to move away from the upright look that Sam Snead, Byron Nelson, and Jimmy Demaret, among others, had. For some years he encouraged a whole generation of golfers to follow his example; he was far and away the most influential golfer of his day, so it's not surprising that there was a general trend to swing the club on a flattish plane. Then a new hero, Jack Nicklaus, came along during the early 1960s and influenced golfers to swing more upright.

There was another interesting feature of

Hogan's swing—specifically, his backswing. Technically, it could have been termed a "reverse pivot". A golfer reverse pivots when he does not get the majority of his weight onto his right side at the top of the backswing. This creates a situation where his body appears to be leaning somewhat left toward the target, and is often referred to as "hanging on the left side." Hogan had this look. He wasn't affected to any large degree, however, because he coiled and stretched so well during his backswing motion; and in his case this motion did not require a substantial weight transfer. He was, as one could call it, "centered" at the top. His upper body appeared to be centered or on top of the ball, while his hips leaned toward the target. (High-handicappers who have a severe reverse pivot often get both their hips and shoulders leaning toward the target.)

Hogan's centered position occurred as a result of the combination of his flat swing

Most players need to "load" their weight into the right side and get "behind" the ball.

pivot, is that from the top of the swing the golfer's weight moves in the opposite direction to what it should—back to the right side as opposed to the left side as the club approaches impact. Hence the term "reverse pivot."

Power is dissipated in a severe reverse pivot as the golfer releases the club too early; that is, well before the ball is struck. The club decelerates at impact, which is obviously not what we want to happen. On the other hand, loading up into the right side going back encourages the weight to return to the left side on the downswing, thereby promoting an accelerated release of the clubhead through the ball. Hogan, because of his build and athleticism, was able to find a way to swing the club dynamically and repetitively, despite what could be considered a technical flaw. His reverse pivot actually gave him some extra leverage on the downswing, but more on that in the next chapter. This only goes to show that what suits one golfer does not necessarily suit another, and that golfers should in most cases avoid trying to copy a player's swing in all its details, or even in its overall look. These elements are more than details or a general look. They are often uniquely personal characteristics and movements, and it can be a grave mistake to think they can be applied beyond the individual.

plane, tucked right elbow, ultra-steady head, and the fact that his left knee, when he was hitting a shot (as opposed to posing for a photograph), shot out toward the ball rather than behind it. A number of today's players stay fairly centered and don't get fully into their right sides; Jose Maria Olazabal, the two-time Masters winner, is one example. But for most players, a reverse pivot is ruinous. I feel that it is far preferable to aggressively "load" up the weight into the right side so as to assist in the coiling process; this is especially the case with the longer clubs, where the feeling is that you are "behind" the ball. Leaning with the body (hips or shoulders) toward the target, or allowing the weight to "hang" significantly on the left side at the top of the backswing can lead to a weak, choppy downswing for high-handicappers, or a compensation of some sort for better players. The problem, especially with a reverse

The most striking image in the annals of golf instruction is of Hogan addressing the ball with his head through a hole in a pane of glass. Hogan's discussion of the plane has played a major role in golf instruction for forty years. He, in effect, introduced a new way of looking at the swing. Every teacher discusses swing plane today; it would be unthinkable to ignore the subject.

However, swing plane discussion can get complicated and confusing because many different planes influence the consistency of a swing: there are shaft, clubface, wrist, arms, and shoulder planes. Hogan focused on the shoulders, left arm and club all moving on the same plane, which was pure Hoganism. One must remember that Hogan, with an erect posture and little forward bend from the hips, was set up to turn his shoulders on a very horizontal plane; this contributed greatly to his "flat" look. While this address position certainly was instrumental in creating his plane, so, equally, was the way in which he rotated his left forearm in a clockwise fashion on the backswing. He rotated his shoulders and left arm so that they were parallel to each other at the top of his swing; a line drawn through his left arm at the top would be parallel to a line drawn through his shoulders at the top. Forearm rotation is a very subtle movement, and is not easily observable even with a camera. Nevertheless, I feel that it was an integral part of Hogan's swing, even though, for reasons unknown to me, he did not mention it in his book. However, he did refer to the rotation of his left arm for a June 1985 story in *Golf Digest*. "My left arm swung right across my chest on the backswing," Hogan said. He carried on with this thought when he said, "The idea is to rotate the club with the left arm." Clearly, this rotation was a significant element in Hogan's backswing. At the same time, developing a flatter, more compact backswing, even with a weaker grip, still did not entirely stop his hooking problems.

### The "Secret"

A flat swing plane normally exaggerates a hooking problem by encouraging the club to move on an even shallower inside-to-out path when approaching the ball. This was very evident in Hogan's case because when he made an actual swing (not so much when he posed for a photograph), it was noticeable that the club was well "laid off" or pointed to the left of the target at the top of his backswing. This laid-off look really accentuates an in-to-out swing for a good player who has a strong lower body move to start the downswing. As Hogan got older his backswing shortened—as happens with many players—and his club became even more laid off. This backswing, in combination with his speed of movement down and the late hit—where the clubhead lagged far behind the hands—still produced a hook at

times, despite his swing changes and weaker grip. He searched desperately for a way to counteract this problem. As he wrote in the August 8, 1955 issue of *Life* magazine, "I had a low, ducking, agonizing hook, the kind you can hang your coat on. When it caught the rough it was the terror of the field mice." Through his perseverance he finally found a way to counteract and cure his hook. The answer was his "secret."

But what was that secret when Hogan finally revealed it to an expectant golfing world in the aforementioned issue of *Life* magazine? It happened like this: frustrated by his inability to find a solution while on the tournament trail, he packed his bags and went home. There he all but isolated himself for a few days to think about things and see if he could come up with some ideas. After much thought and after wracking his brain it suddenly came to him— a key that the old Scottish pros used. Hogan

Hogan's laid-off look increased the likelihood that he would hit a hook.

Hogan's secret: cupping the left wrist at the top got the toe of the club hanging down in an open position. The result? A fade.

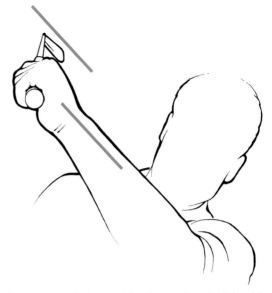

The position that Hogan achieved naturally: a flat left wrist, a squarer clubface (lying parallel to the wrist and forearm).

jumped up with excitement at his new discovery and the promise it offered, and went out to hit some balls. And lo and behold, it worked. He hit some soft, feathery fades, and instinctively, he knew he had it. He had found the cure. No matter how hard he hit the ball, it would not go left. "The harder I hit it," Hogan said, "the better it worked. There was no loss of distance." Now he knew he was really onto something.

The secret, in my opinion, was this: Combined with his weak grip, Hogan focused on "cupping" his left wrist as he approached the top of his backswing; the cup was apparent in the cover photograph of *Life* magazine's August 8, 1955 issue. This "cupping" of the wrist in combination with rotating his left arm clockwise, in effect producing a real pronation of the wrist, got the toe of his club hanging down more to the ground and the face in a very open position, as opposed to a square position with the clubface looking more toward the sky. From this open position at the top, he was able to keep the clubface from being closed at impact, no matter how hard he rotated his left

arm or tried to close the face coming down (a move that normally tends to shut the face excessively by the time the clubhead reaches the ball).

Hogan had finally found what he had sought for so long, but why had he waited nearly a decade before letting the world in on his secret? The answer was simple, and he expressed it straightforwardly. "Now that I am through with serious competition—and I worked harder getting ready for this last Open [the 1955 United States Open] than any tournament in my life— I don't mind letting the world in on my secret." The open clubface meant that he was able, no matter how hard he hit the ball or how shallowly he came into it, to produce solid left to right softly-landing shots time after time. He stated that the cupping feeling at the top was one of his really conscious moves in the swing. For a draw he would just forget about the "cup" and swing normally, thereby keeping the left wrist fairly flat and the clubface much squarer (parallel to the wrist and forearm). This position produced a right-to-left ball flight. The millions of golfers who waited patiently for his secret were probably disappointed, thinking that maybe Hogan's secret would open the door for them to long-lasting great golf. However, there was another secret in Hogan's *Life* magazine article.

"I doubt if it (the secret) will be worth a doggone to the weekend duffer and it will ruin a bad golfer," Hogan wrote toward the end of the article. "With the clubface so wide open at the top of the backswing anybody who fails to close it properly on the way down will push the ball off to the right—or worse yet, shank it off to the right at a horrible right angle. But it will be a blessing to the good golfer." Maybe this was the truly important secret: only better players should even think of trying the secret, while all others should ignore it.

Hogan's secret of cupping the left wrist and getting the clubface more open would be absolutely ruinous for the slicing population who would give anything to hit a big hook and keep the ball out of the right-hand rough. Golfers who slice the ball would only exacerbate their problem by trying to adopt the Hogan secret. This is probably the reason he didn't mention it in *Five Lessons*. However, that didn't stop people who had read about the secret in *Life* magazine from turning themselves inside-out while trying his secret. I've talked to any number of golfers who tried the secret when Hogan revealed it, only to experience nothing but frustration.

Let's get back to the plane and the pane of glass. The angle of the pane of glass that Hogan visualized meant that both the shoulders and the arms brushed against the glass; they moved on parallel planes. I maintain that at the top, most players, especially taller ones and players with limited flexibility, would benefit from an arm plane slightly steeper or more upright than the shoulder plane, as opposed to Hogan's parallel left arm and shoulder look. In my view it feels and looks less restricted (the club is more on line—pointing to the target at the top). It provides room for the arms to swing down to

Hogan's parallel left arm and shoulder look.

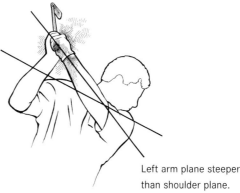

Left arm plane steeper than shoulder plane.

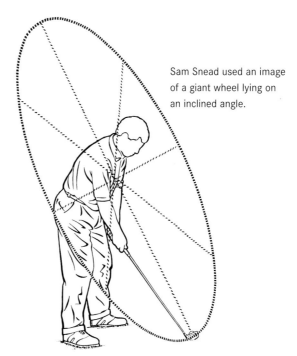

Sam Snead used an image of a giant wheel lying on an inclined angle.

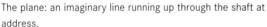
The plane: an imaginary line running up through the shaft at address.

Shaft steeper than original line at halfway-back position.

impact without the body obstructing their movement. Still, the pane of glass does provide an image of the overall inclined shape of the swing and its angle—neither vertical nor horizontal but somewhere in between—and is fairly similar to the picture Sam Snead uses to picture the swing—that of an inclined wheel.

It's been my experience that most golfers find it more helpful to visualize the plane of the swing as a line running up through the clubshaft as it sits at address, rather than the pane of glass running through the shoulders. This image is clearer to my students than the pane of glass. Use this line at address as a reference and try to return the shaft on a similar, even matching, plane at impact. If you can do that consistently, how you do it is irrelevant. I might add that Snead often advises golfers to think of only one thing in the swing: returning

to impact in the same position they were in at address. Over the years I have had great success in getting my students to return their club into the correct slot at impact by having them swing the club on a backswing plane that is slightly steeper or more upright than the angle it was on at address. The golfer who applies dynamic body motion along with this slightly steeper backswing plane will more easily be able to shallow the shaft back onto its proper plane coming down. Gravity plays its part as the club changes direction, so having it on this slightly more upright or steeper plane encourages it to fall on a flatter or shallower plane coming down. Some players may even feel that there is a slight inside loop as the club drops, which is much more desirable than an outside loop where the shaft plane gets very steep coming down—typical of poorer players.

Shaft shallows on downswing to get back on a line parallel to the original position.

Shaft returns to the same plane at impact.

This slightly steeper-to-shallower move works better for most people because it is easier to do this than to try to swing the club machine-like up and down on the same backswing and downswing plane. We are not like the club testing machines where one lever is linked to a fixed axis that produces a symmetrical up and down plane and hits the identical shot time after time. Given the human element and factoring in all the moving parts and joints in the body, I think it makes sense to build in a little margin for error. This is why I prefer the steeper-to-shallower look; it's not a substantial shift from what Hogan advised, but certainly it does represent a shift. Even though Hogan himself spoke about shallowing the plane on the downswing, to all intents and purposes he really came close to swinging on one plane back and forth. This approach sounds simple in practice, but in reality it is difficult for many players. The majority of tour players have a steeper-to-shallower look.

In every golf swing there is a varying amount of inward, rounded, and upward movement of the club, and golfers need to be aware of these movements. The different shapes and looks during the swing occur because we are standing to the side of the ball with the club at an inclined angle, and swinging it on an elliptical orbit. Golf isn't like baseball where one effectively swings on a more or less horizontal plane. The golf swing motion is more complex and offers endless variations of the plane, which is why any discussion of plane can be confusing. The crucial plane is the one coming into impact. Many skilled players are able through compensations and practice to get into a good downswing plane despite having either a super-upright or ultra-flat backswing plane.

Swing planes vary from player to player, even among golfers of similar heights. Some tall players have flattish swings, while some short players use upright swings. One shape of plane is not necessarily better than another, because many that look technically flawed do produce good results.

Hogan himself noted that planes vary depending on build. He was able to develop a flat backswing plane and then match it with a downswing plane that traced nearly the same path in the opposite direction. As I have suggested with respect to other areas of the swing, make sure that you repeat whichever backswing plane you decide to use. The swing is a chain reaction and so the quality of your downswing is going to depend on how consistently you repeat your backswing.

The proof of whether your backswing is right for you or not will be reflected in the quality of your ball-striking. Johnny Miller has said that the ultimate proof of whether a golfer has some good things in his swing is the flight of the ball; that is, whether the ball flies in the direction and with the trajectory and shape you choose. I couldn't agree more.

### To Become an 80-Breaker—or Better

Hogan focused on the importance of sequential movement during the start of the backswing—the hands, arms, shoulders, and hips moving in that order. Sequence is obviously important as the club is moved away. There are many ways to spoil the sequence, and set off a cascade of problems. Some examples: one golfer may rotate the hips too fast, another might roll the clubhead away at the start using the hands only, without involving the shoulders and chest. A third might lift the club straight up with the hands and arms without allowing the trunk to join the action, etc., etc. These independent and out-of-sequence moves disrupt rhythm and timing, and therefore reduce power and accuracy. It is critical in building a swing that every golfer understands that it consists of two basic components: the body turn and the

This drill will help you become aware of how your body should work during the backswing. (continued on next page)

arm swing. Good rhythm is created when these components jell. An observer can sense this rhythm and see a flow. Hogan made note of the fact that in the full swing the body carries the arms and hands rather than the other way round; I refer to this as the "dog wagging the tail." That's the meaning of the phrase "passive hands" that we often hear. "Passive hands" does not mean "dead" hands; it simply means that they transmit the power through to the clubhead from the body and are not the source of power.

**Try this simple drill to become aware of how your body should work. Take up your posture with a club in hand; now drop the club to the ground and fold your arms across your midsection. Keeping your lower body solid and without extraneous foot, knee, and hip motion, move and turn into your right side. Feel the left shoulder moving "down, back, and across," so that, as**

Hogan says, you feel the left shoulder brushing your chin. The shoulders should turn at ninety degrees to your spine; make sure you don't tilt or raise them appreciably. Hogan's flat look was created by his fairly horizontal shoulder turn, but at the same time he still turned them perpendicular to his erect spine. A small inward movement with your left knee is fine, and even a slight raising of the left heel is okay, depending on your flexibility. But keep a reasonable gap between both knees at the top, because this produces a stable base around which you can wind up. Just remember that your right knee position is the governor of your movement, as Hogan acknowledges. At the top, keep it in the same position as it was at address; keep it flexed and solid.

By doing this you will not have to consciously retard or "restrain" the hip movement to get wound up, as Hogan put it. I prefer players to focus on the 'gap' and on anchoring the right knee as keys to stabilize the lower body and to achieve a coiled position at the top of the backswing. I think it's all but impossible, and very uncomfortable, to curtail the turn of the hips while at the same time trying to turn the shoulders fully; there's a relationship between them, after all, and only a very flexible person could try to do this. Hogan was certainly flexible, but it is apparent in photographs of him that he turned his hips far more than he thought he did. The old thought of plus or minus 90 degrees for the shoulder turn and plus or minus 45 degrees for the hip turn is still a good rule to follow.

Let's now consider the "fixed-head syndrome." I feel most players would be better off if they allowed their heads to move a little laterally as they turn on the backswing, especially with the

Doing this isometric drill will give you the feel of width, coil and extension at the top of the backswing.

Many players should feel the butt end of the club moving away first, even in an exaggerated manner, as Hogan is showing here.

longer clubs. This is conducive to the golfer getting the weight loaded up and behind the ball at the top. Staying too centered can cause a reverse pivot, as we have seen with respect to Hogan. This is not a desirable position for most players. The preferable position is a full coil allied to a complete windup with the torso (from the navel up to the shoulders). A modest head movement will often help. Allow your chin to rotate to the right, which will promote this head movement. As a checkpoint at the top of your backswing, try to get your shirt buttons positioned on top of your right leg, and your left shoulder behind your left hip. It is perfectly okay if your chin swivels, enabling your head to move an inch or two on the backswing, especially with the driver. This motion encourages a complete turn and really benefits senior golfers and anybody who needs to get his weight more into his right side. As an added feeling, sense you are looking at the ball out of your left eye at the top of the swing. Please note: as long as the right knee remains stable you will have no problems with swaying.

**To gain further benefit from the arms-folded drill, I'd like you to do the following variation so that you can feel where your arms should be relative to your shoulders at the top of the swing. Simply extend your left arm and hook the pocket of your right elbow underneath your left elbow. Your left arm should be fairly straight and you should feel a stretching in the upper back and a tugging sensation in the left shoulder. Hold this isometric position for a few seconds. It will provide you with a keen awareness for the top position (width, coil, and extension). This is an excellent exercise for muscle memory and also for loosening up prior to playing or practicing. Do this drill a few times a day to develop the correct muscular feelings. It's the best way to translate theory into feeling, and then into practice while hitting shots.**

As you practice the proper positions and feelings, you will eventually find that they have worked themselves instinctively into your swing. Realize, however, that when you

Move the butt end of the club first to start the backswing.

do make the decision to work on your swing you will initially exert a fair amount of conscious thought in order to develop a repeating motion—this is to be expected, and is part of the learning process. Without question the easiest areas for you to be conscious of are the address and start. One is able to control movements and positions early in the swing; this is not so much the case in the later stages.

*Here's a sound way to start the backswing after completing the waggle—either Hogan's or a variation that I will suggest at the end of this chapter. I have found this a superb means of getting the sequence of motion started. Move the butt end— the top end—of the club first.* The real swingwrecker at the start of the swing is an accentuated movement with the clubhead only— picking it up, fanning it, etc.—without the unit of the hands, clubhead, and arms moving in

unison. This mistake gets the swing off track right away. However, moving the butt end gets things started away together at a nice pace. In his early years Hogan not only did this but he did it in an exaggerated manner, as did many of his contemporaries.

You will probably feel that the clubhead gets a little closed going away, as Hogan's looked, even with his revamped swing. He often said that he tried to open the clubface as soon as he took the club away, but it never really looked that way. He would move the triangle (the club, hands, and arms) initially in one piece to about a third of the way into the backswing, and then with his very quick tempo he would simultaneously cock his wrists and rotate his left arm and clubface open onto a flattish inside plane. My recommendation to most players is that they not consciously rotate the

Left elbow pointing down—shaft plane steeper—minimal rotation.

Left arm rotated, indicating shallower plane.

Butt end of the club points within the golden triangle.

face open once they have moved the triangle away. Golfers, particularly those who slice the ball, should, conversely, limit arm and club rotation and keep the left elbow pointing to the ground as long as possible. An important checkpoint in the swing in my opinion is the halfway-back spot where the left arm is parallel to the ground—this position is really the top of the backswing minus the turn.

Pointing the left elbow down accomplishes two significant things: it helps set the club on a more upright plane halfway back (which I favor for high-handicap players) and also sets the face in a square-to-slightly-closed position, which is ideal if you are trying to rid yourself of a slice. This is where "different strokes for different folks" comes in, because if you are a lower-handicap player or need to flatten your backswing plane, then it may well be in your best interest to subtly rotate the left arm, once you have moved the triangle away. The above illustrations showing the location of the orange dots on the arms reflect these thoughts. Additionally, you may even want to experiment with Hogan's secret of "cupping" and opening the face as you near the top—after you have rotated your left arm—if you are a genuine hooker of the ball. I would just advise you to do things gradually and to monitor the swing closely, possibly with the use of a video camera and a mirror, but also by letting your ball

flight provide your feedback. Some trial and error is involved. Just make sure you hit some practice balls before you try it on the course.

**You should also be aware of a couple of other points at this stage. As always, it helps to incorporate a drill. In this case, choke down halfway on the club and swing back to what I feel is the important halfway-back checkpoint of your backswing where the left arm is parallel to the ground and the wrists are almost fully cocked or set.**

**First point: see that the butt end of the club points somewhere within the area of the golden triangle, as I refer to it, the base of which is measured from a point at the ball/target line to a midway position between the feet and the ball. Any point slightly inside the ball/target line indicates a shaft swing plane steeper than the original position—most beneficial for many players. Hogan pointed the butt end of the club almost directly at the ball/target line. I see many**

Many players get the club too flat halfway back.

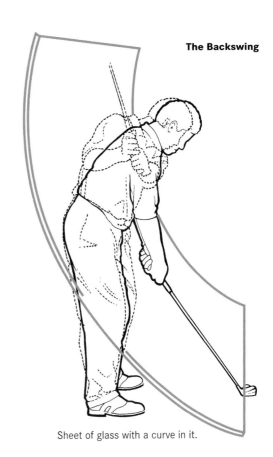

Sheet of glass with a curve in it.

poor players who whip the club around them going back, and point the butt end way beyond and above the target line, which puts the club on too flat a plane at this halfway-back stage (above). The player who gets into this awkward position is then forced to lift and raise his arms steeply to complete his backswing. Getting too flat too early, then, often results in too upright a position at the top of the backswing, and frequently produces an overswing and a complete lack of coil.

I have concluded after having taught thousands of lessons that a more helpful image than the pane of glass up through the neck is one where a golfer is standing within a sheet of glass which has a curve in it. This concave image is ideal for the backswing because the curve in the glass represents the slight steepening of the plane.

**Second point: check to see that at the halfway-back point your hands are positioned**

Hogan's "deep" hand position halfway back as compared to hands positioned more in front of the chest.

Jack Nicklaus's flying or "floating" right elbow.

Right forearm parallel to spine at the top of the swing.

approximately opposite the middle of your chest. In my experience the image of the pane of glass that Hogan uses tends to set the golfer's hands too deeply across the chest; that is, too far around and behind it. This can once again lead to the golfer lifting the arms to complete the backswing, ultimately arriving in a non-coiled, steep position at the top—the position Hogan abhors. Keeping the hands more in front of your chest will allow you to move from the halfway-back position up to the perfect "slot" at the top simply by completing your shoulder turn—the ideal way to complete the backswing.

Now we're approaching the top of the back-swing. This statement might sound strong, but forget about the tucked right elbow position that Hogan achieved and advocated, and that many players have tried to copy. Instruction has taken this idea too far. The majority of players who tuck the right elbow down completely lose all width and extension—the components of a maximum swing arc—and also distance. The only exception regarding the tucked right elbow would be the player who is ultra-supple and who is able to create a lot of coil, and for whatever reason is working on a flat swing plane.

Hogan, with his flexibility and with very little bulk to his chest, was one of these players. He was able to create a tucked, flat, compact look. Jack Nicklaus, on the other hand, has a much bigger chest and had to allow his arms to separate from his torso, getting his hands high. This led to Nicklaus's famous flying right elbow, which we have seen and read about for years, and which theorists seeking a sort of purity in the swing have often criticized. His build and flexibility determined his upright arm position and "floating" right elbow, as I call it. Only in this way could he wind up and complete his backswing. Indeed, a floating right elbow is not a problem as long as you do not force it up in the air, and as long as the elbow drops into the proper slot on the down-swing. Other successful players who follow the Nicklaus model are Fred Couples and John Daly. Couples is an extremely long hitter who allows his right elbow to float, which, in part, accounts for the extraordinary freedom and flow that mark his powerful swing. And then there's Daly, the longest driver in modern-day tournament golf, whose brawny, flexible frame supports a huge turn, a big overswing of the club, and a high right elbow. His first move down, though, returns the club into a perfect slot.

Tucking the right elbow down in most cases reduces width and coil, and dates back to the days of whippy hickory shafts, when players were advised to keep the elbow close in so they could control the shafts. I have found that a valuable checkpoint at the top is to ensure that your right forearm approximately parallels your spine. You won't go far wrong from here. The right arm blends nicely with the plane of the left arm. Remember, though, that build and posture play a major role in the overall look of a swing. Consider the tall player who has a greater degree of forward bend in his upper body; if this person has short arms then he will turn his shoulders on a more tilted axis, still perpendicular to his spine. This will naturally result in a more upright look to his swing plane.

As far as the ideal wrist and clubface position, I have spoken about Hogan's weak grip, his secret of cupping his left wrist and allowing the toe of the clubhead to hang down at the top of his backswing to fight his hook. In general, as I said in the hands chapter, I believe you should place your left hand at address in a fairly neutral position where approximately two knuckles are showing, making a slight cup appear at the base of the wrist. The idea is to retain this look as you swing to the top. Make sure that the clubface is parallel to your left forearm and wrist at the top, in what is normally viewed as a square position (or at least as near to parallel as you can get it). Ensure also that the hint of the cup seen in the wrist at address is still visible. Maintaining the look from address to the top will technically put you in a square or neutral position up there, and one that you theoretically

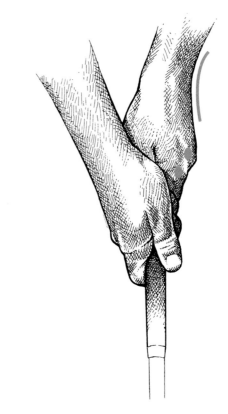

Neutral grip: two knuckles showing, slight cup at base of left wrist visible.

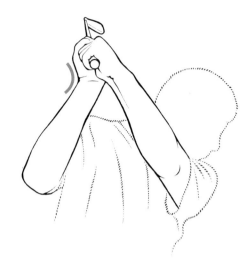

Neutral position of the grip is maintained to the top, where a slight cup is still visible.

Right wrist in a cupped position at the top benefits many amateurs who are weak hitters or slicers.

reach without any manipulation of the club-face, wrists, and hands. In all honesty, though, I learned long ago that ideal positions and theories are just that—theories. You have to find out what works. Many players do not achieve the so-called "ideal," yet they get the job done. Hogan himself manipulated the club to the top.

*I would offer a suggestion, however, to those golfers who are weak hitters or slice the ball. I suggest that from the halfway-back position I have described, with the left elbow pointing down, you swing to the top while getting your right wrist under the shaft in a cupped position; this might be your secret.* Your left wrist will have a straight or bowed appearance. The clubface will look more toward the sky. I have found this strong position benefits many amateurs. For one thing it firms up the swing, and it also makes it difficult for them to open the clubface coming down; a squarer or closed clubface results in much more solid ball contact. Golfers who have a tough time breaking 80 typically get the face too open on the downswing and have a tough time squaring it up at impact. It's worth trying.

**Curiously, in line with Ben Hogan's swing of**

**fifty years ago, part of the modern look is that players tend to have a full shoulder turn with a fairly short arm swing—a look I favor because it helps eliminate excessive motion. Think in terms of a three-quarter length arm swing and being fully wound up. Hogan certainly took on this look as his swing became more efficient. Once you have established the feel, you will want to confirm and reconfirm it in your subconscious. While using a mirror, practice swinging back to this position so that you can repeat it at will. It's a strong position from which to begin the journey back to the ball. In general, then, a shorter swing will for most players be just as powerful, if not more so, and will be easier to repeat because less can go wrong.**

Finally, let's give some thought to the waggle. Hogan's waggle was usually very brisk because he swung with a quick tempo. Certainly a golfer's tempo is based largely upon his mannerisms, temperament, and general motion. Justin Leonard moves at a measured and deliberate pace; his waggle reflects this pace. Tom Watson and Nick Price move quickly; their waggles are sharp. Some people move, talk, and act quickly, while others do so at a more leisurely pace, and their swings reflect that pace, which

An exaggerated long waggle in which Hogan demonstrates that he likes to feel the clubface open.

is exactly as one would expect. I do feel, contrary to popular thinking, that many people actually try to swing too slowly, especially as a result of trying to slot or "think" the club into specific positions. Remember that the swing is an instinctive motion. It is also true that a golfer who swings too slowly going back can easily rush from the top down—the old adage of "hitting from the top." Many golfers could make their tempo slightly more upbeat, so long as everything moves away smoothly, in synch, and they don't snatch or jerk the club away from the ball. The key is to develop a flowing move, especially at the start and at the point where you change direction; the waggle is a big help toward achieving this desirable situation.

Because Hogan was so intent on getting the clubface open on his backswing, his waggle in my estimation mirrored his thoughts. His key of the right elbow touching the right hip and the left elbow rotating out created for him a mini-version of his backswing. He was acutely aware, because of his hooking problems, of getting the face open and in fact keeping it open throughout his swing. This can be seen in the above photograph, as he demonstrates what he was trying to feel by using an exaggerated, long waggle. However, if you follow the Scottish adage, dating back to before the turn of the century, "as ye waggle so shall ye swing," then many players, apart from severe hookers of the ball or those who for one reason or another get the club shut on the backswing, would do well to adopt a different style of waggle than did Hogan.

You might want to try something along the following lines: after having assumed your address position, with the club hovering above the ground, focus your eyes on the target. In conjunction with your weight moving slightly from left foot to right foot and then back to the left to establish some body motion and rhythm with your feet, move the butt end of the club away a short distance—about six inches, maximum, along the swing path, almost feeling that you are adding more cup in your left wrist as you do it. Feel the left arm building up pressure on your chest. Pause slightly. Now, focusing your eyes back to the ball while maintaining the flow and keeping the hands and arms soft, repeat the motion once more, including the slight weight shift from foot to foot. (Basically, early on, you are synchronizing the body motion with that of the arms and club.) Pause slightly again at the ball, and then, after a subtle bump forward with your knees and hips toward the target, start the butt end away to get the swing into motion. Keep the arms relaxed and "soft" the whole time. The beat is very much like this: one waggle, two waggle, forward, and go. Again, one waggle, two waggle, forward, and go. This isn't a bad mantra for developing the beat to start the swing. It's similar to a server in tennis bouncing the ball and rocking his body to get into rhythm.

This routine can vary. You might want to take an extra waggle, for example, or you might want to come up with one entirely your own. You might not want to look at the target and instead focus on the ball—you can experiment, because, to be sure, any waggle done regularly is better than none. You need something to get yourself into motion.

I have found that my suggested waggle procedure works well for many players. Hogan suggests one way and I'm suggesting another. If you don't feel comfortable with either of these, try to develop one yourself. The whole point of the waggle is that when you look at the target you keep from getting ball-bound; you become focused on the shot at hand. I like the idea of taking two waggles because it shortens thinking time and reduces tension.

The waggle helps synchronize body motion with the movement of the arms and club.

In a nutshell, find a waggle with which you are comfortable and do it over and over at home or on the practice tee so that when you go out and play it becomes an instinctive part of your swing. If you can develop this waggle you'll be amazed at how your consistency improves. Look around and see how few amateurs have anything that resembles a consistent preshot motion—if there is movement, it's generally more of a nervous twitch. And watch the pros. Each may have a different look to his or her waggle, and in fact some players may move the club just to get away from a static position. But the common denominator among better golfers is that they waggle consistently and instinctively, and they do it on every shot.

**Finally, here's one of my favorite drills to help you get your backswing into a groove and incorporate the ideas I've suggested. I use this drill all the time for all types of players. Take a club in your hands with fairly light grip pressure and relaxed arms, then place it just above the ball and ahead of it a couple of feet, slightly inside the target line. From this position you simply swing the club back to the top and hit the shot in the normal manner. You create momentum when you start forward of the ball; this gets you off to a really flowing start. You will feel the grip going first and the clubhead lagging ever so slightly—a lot of freedom and flow without much thought. The wrists cock naturally and easily through the weight and momentum of the club; your trunk is in motion, and the club seems to find the correct plane instinctively. It all adds up to a smooth transition into the downswing and an accelerated release of the club through impact. Try this initially with some teed-up 7-irons, and then work on some longer clubs; you will establish the feel and rhythm you need to start the swing and to get the club into that all-important "slot" at the top. Doing this drill really does help when you get tense at address because of thinking too much or being too position-conscious in your swing. Incorporate it into your practice session. It will be of great help.**

Club forward of the ball to start backswing drill.

# THE DOWNSWING

Ben Hogan gained deep satisfaction when he made flush contact with the ball, especially when it travelled on his intended line and trajectory. Certainly, all golfers crave the feeling sent up from the club to the hands and into the body when they make such contact. However, even the greatest players are unable to hit the ball solidly every time. The great Walter Hagen, one of golf's most charismatic players and a five-time PGA Championship winner, said he expected to hit six or seven bad shots in a round. Hagen was one of the most solid ball-strikers of his day, yet he still felt this way. Bobby Jones wrote that absolute consistency is impossible in golf. Hogan himself acknowledged that he only hit one or two shots a round that came off exactly as he planned them. In reality, the best players build swings that produce playable misses — the fewer the misses, and the

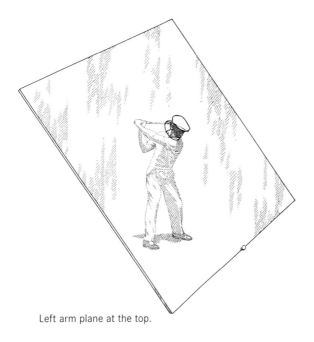

Left arm plane at the top.

Hogan's image of the downswing is that its plane lies on a flatter angle than that of the backswing—as a result the base of the downswing plane shifts to the right of the target line thus encouraging an in-to-out swing path.

better the misses are, the more consistent a player becomes. In this chapter, we will discuss the part of the swing during which the player hits the ball: the downswing.

The backswing plane that Hogan subscribed to will, he emphasized, develop a repetitive swing. As we now know, he spoke of the backswing plane as inclining on an imaginary line that runs from the ball up to the shoulders and beyond. If the golfer rotates his shoulders and swings his arms and club back on this plane, then at the top his left arm, including his forearm and a flat left wrist, will be extended at an angle to the ball that is identical to the plane line. The other elements that the golfer must take into account at the top of the backswing are: his right elbow has to fold down correctly, his left arm should be properly extended but not stiff, his shoulder turn must be complete, and his hands have to cock naturally. (Remember: Hogan did not make mention of his secret in *Five Lessons*; he did not, therefore, talk about

the cupping of the left wrist.) Keeping the pane of glass in mind, Hogan's contention is that the shoulders, arms and hands, which lie below the glass, will then be perfectly positioned to move down in a repeating, synchronized manner.

As mentioned in the previous chapter, Hogan believed that the downswing plane differs somewhat from the backswing plane. It lies on a flatter, less steeply inclined path. This lower pitch is created automatically when the golfer turns his hips to the left, which lowers the right shoulder. Consequently, the image of the pane of glass must be altered. It now lies on a slightly shallower angle, and its base points a little to the right of the target. This promotes a more in-to-out shape to the swing. Hogan felt that the golfer shouldn't pay undue attention to this altered downswing plane (although it's important to have a concept of it in mind) but rather on the things that encourage it to occur.

The hips start the downswing by turning to

Hips, shoulders, arms, and hands release their power carrying Hogan through to the finish.

the left, an idea that Hogan introduced in *Power Golf*. When done properly, this move practically guarantees a first-class move back to the ball. The movement creates speed and weight transfer, while clearing the hips at the proper time allows the golfer to swing his arms freely though the impact area. A slight lateral motion accompanies this turning of the hips back to the ball so that the golfer can transfer weight to the left foot. Hogan cautioned that even with a big shoulder turn, if there is too much hip turn during the backswing, not enough tension is built up and there is nothing to start the hips forward on the downswing. The basic rule is that the greater the tension or stretch, the more rapidly a player can move the hips to start the downswing. In Hogan's opinion, the faster the hips turn, the better.

As happens in the early part of the backswing, the hip action on the downswing starts a chain reaction. The weight moves smoothly to the left leg, and the right knee kicks in

toward the target. The multiplying power generated by the synchronized motion of the torso, hips and shoulders transfers the power down through the arms, then into the hands, and finally it is multiplied again into the clubhead as it swings aggressively through the ball.

The one sure way to destroy the powerful multiplying factor of the torso, Hogan believed, is to start the downswing with the hands. This forces the body out and over, which produces an outside-in swing. The results are all too apparent to golfers; they hit weak slices and pulls. To counteract this, Hogan cautioned novices and average golfers to keep conscious hand action out of the swing. He contended that the hands really do nothing on the downswing until the arms have dropped into a position just above hip height. The arms get there because the motion of the hips carries them down. Hogan says that the golfer, by swinging the club up to the top, holding the position, and then moving the hips back to the left, can feel this. It's immediately noticeable that the hands and arms drop automatically without the golfer having to think about it. At this stage of the swing there should also be a sensation of stored-up power. One's only thought from this point on, Hogan felt, was to hit the ball, not to steer the clubface. Hogan's action was noted for being a continuous motion from the start of the downswing to the end of the follow-through.

Hogan said repeatedly that, while playing, he thought of only two things regarding the downswing: he thought of starting the hips first, and of hitting the ball as hard as possible with the body, arms and hands, in that sequence. He felt that not much could go wrong for the golfer who produced the correct sequence of events during the swing. Hogan's own swing proved that this proper chain reaction produces explosive power.

Although Hogan thought of only two things concerning the downswing, he felt it was a good idea for the golfer to understand what the hands and arms do in the all-important impact area.

Hogan believes the hips carry the arms down. To observe this, swing to the top and hold the position. Now move the left hip and notice how the hands and arms have dropped.

The motion of the right arm in the golf swing is similar to the underhanded sidearm throw in baseball.

To understand the correct motion of the right hand and arm, Hogan advised the golfer to think of a baseball infielder throwing the ball in an underhanded, sidearm fashion. As the arm swings forward, the right elbow is close to the hip and the elbow leads the arm. Eventually, the forearm and hand catch up with the elbow and the arm is fairly straight when it releases the ball. As the follow-through of the throw takes place, the wrist and hand rotate over and the palm points downward at the finish. This is a very similar motion to the one that occurs during the hitting segment in the golf swing. The mechanics of this throwing motion is apparent in all the great swingers before and after Hogan: Jones, Sarazen, Snead, Nelson, Nicklaus and Tiger Woods today.

On full shots, Hogan wanted to hit the ball as hard as he could with his right hand, without it overpowering the left. He felt that the benefit of this two-handed action was that it kept the left hand driving continuously as well. He also paid attention to the fact that coming into impact, the left wrist and the back of the left hand began to gradually supinate. That is, they rotate from nearly a palm-down position at the top of the swing (knuckles pointing up), toward more of a palm-up position coming into the ball (knuckles beginning to point down). At impact, the back of the left hand faces toward the target. The wrist bone is raised, too, as Hogan is showing here (above right); the result is that when the clubhead contacts the ball, the wrist bone is nearer the target than any other part of the hand. In this position, the left wrist won't interrupt the power flow and the right hand won't take over.

Hogan wished he had as many as three right hands to pour on the power at this stage of the swing, as long as his left hand remained in control. According to him, every good golfer is in a supinating position at impact, while every poor golfer does just the opposite—he pronates. That is, he flips the wrists in an attempt to manipulate the clubhead, believing this will square the clubface at impact. But in doing so,

Left wrist supination.

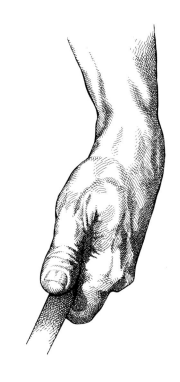

Slightly convex supinated left wrist: ideal, in Hogan's opinion.

Pronated, concave left wrist, as seen with poor players.

Supination helps develop a wide arc and gets the arms fully extended just past impact.

he scoops the ball in the air and loses power. Hogan wrote the following in an April 1956 article in *Golf Digest*. "I've noticed one thing that all good golfers do and all bad golfers do not. The good ones have their left wrist leading at impact. It seems a small thing, but I've found it to be universally true. At impact the left wrist of a good player is slightly convex, while that of a poor player is generally concave."

Supination was important to Hogan as he felt it helps the player maintain a wide arc through the hitting area by encouraging the arms to be fully extended just after impact. It also helps a golfer hit the ball cleanly and solidly and control the trajectory, especially with the irons, because the clubhead will automatically strike the ball and then the turf. This action produces a piercing flight in which the ball bores through the air.

Ben Hogan believed the golfer should be aware of some other points regarding the impact zone. At impact, the right arm is gradually straightening, but is still slightly bent. The only point at which both arms are straight is just after impact, and the supinating left wrist leads them to this position. The left elbow now begins to fold down in a fashion similar to the right elbow on the backswing. The right arm remains extended all the way through to the finish in a mirror image of the left arm on the backswing. At the completion of the follow-through, the left elbow points to the ground, comparable to the way the right elbow did at the top of the backswing. The right shoulder hits the chin, and the shoulders now finally catch up to the hips.

As far as the lower body is concerned, Hogan liked to have his hips opening up towards the

At impact, the right arm is straightening but is still slightly bent.

Left arm folding in the follow-through matches the right arm folding on the backswing.

Right arm during follow-through mirrors the left arm going back.

Left elbow position at the finish resembles the right elbow at the top of the backswing.

target with the left leg bowing outwards and the weight moving to the outside of that foot. His final thought for the downswing was always to hit the ball hard. He felt that many golfers tried to steer the ball on line and curtail their power, thinking that by doing so they are reducing any potential error. His opinion was—and he certainly demonstrated this—that with good fundamentals, the harder one hits the ball, the straighter it would go.

Clearly, Hogan was scrupulous in his attention to detail. He wanted the golfer to understand specific points, and was always very careful to speak and write concisely—and precisely—about the workings and technicalities of the golf swing.

## My View

One could make a strong argument that the triumvirate of Ben Hogan, Sam Snead, and Byron Nelson were the fathers of modern-day golf. Their swings and ball-striking prowess would fit right into the contemporary world of professional golf. They represent the dividing line between the relatively handsy swings of Walter Hagen and later Bobby Jones, whose techniques were based on keeping whippy hickory shafts under control, and the more body-oriented swings which developed as the more consistent steel shafts entered the game. Hogan was very progressive in his thinking, especially in the downswing area, where his general thoughts about the significant role of the lower body have been proven correct by teachers, players, and even biomechanical experts. I do think, however, that some of Hogan's thoughts have been misinterpreted over the years. I also think that what he felt happened during his swing did not always take place the way he described it. In *Let 'er Rip*, Gardner Dickinson comments on Hogan's belief that he had managed to retard his hip turn during his backswing. But, Dickinson writes, "I could never see any restriction or absence of hip turn, especially with the driver." And, further, as Dickinson writes, "In other words, even the greatest don't always swing like they think they do."

It is not surprising, then, that the written record of Hogan's views is misleading in places. Today we have the advantage of high-speed film and other modern technology; it is much easier for us to see more clearly what takes place. But in offering some alternative ideas, I do not want in any way to diminish Hogan's superb ability to analyze how he struck the ball; he was years ahead of his time in thinking about the swing. As far as he was concerned—and you must remember he was a player rather than a teacher, although he did some teaching in his younger years—the thoughts and feelings with which he experimented provided a system that worked beautifully for him.

That system gave Hogan a means of neutralizing his tendency to hook the ball. As a rule, good players and players with athletic ability fight hooks rather than slices. Poorer players with less athleticism tend to hit an uncontrolled slice. Their swings are less dynamic and so they rely on more upper-body motion to start the downswing as a means of creating power. In general, then, the good players overuse their lower bodies while getting the club swinging too much from the inside; they rely on hand action to square the face up, but this can produce hooks and/or pushes if they do not time the release of their hands perfectly. Poorer golfers overuse their shoulders and arms, which produces a steeper, more outside-in swing path that results in slices and pulls.

What is required from a solid top-of-the-backswing position, then, is an effective lower-body action to initiate the downswing. Clearly, it is this action more than any other that will put the club not only on the correct path (back to the ball) but also on the optimum plane. When these two elements harmonize, square-faced contact and solid shots result.

In my opinion, the swing plane Hogan advocates—relatively flat with the hands low at the

Looking down the line and from the target, one can see how far Hogan has swung his club sharply left and inside after impact.

top—can cause some problems. When the better player who incorporates this plane and hand position takes Hogan's advice to start the downswing with an ultra-quick hip rotation, the club tends to fall behind the body. The clubhead very often swings too much from in-to-out, resulting in big hooks or pushes. Even though Hogan's club approached the ball on an extreme inside path, the open clubface that he had created by incorporating his secret enabled him to drag the butt end of the club aggressively left of his body after contact with the ball—probably because of his strong left side. The clubhead essentially then moved sharply inside after impact, mirroring its approach to the ball. Hogan's hands also did not cross over until well after the ball had left the clubface; his divots pointed a touch left of the target and he hit a gentle fade. His shot pattern has been described as one where the ball, upon reach-

ing its apex, fell off a little to the right.

Hogan spoke often about swinging the club in-to-out, but it was not an in-to-out swing in the true sense of the term. Hogan's path was a fairly exaggerated in-to-in motion, or more to the point, from inside the target line to square and then back to inside the target line—square being impact. Let me elaborate. I think there has been far too liberal a use of the term "swinging in-to-out" over the years, especially when it refers to what a slicer needs to do to correct his problem of swinging from out-to-in. Golfers have frequently been advised to "swing out to two o'clock," as if this were a cure-all for a player's problems. But it certainly is not. In-to-out is a throwback to an earlier era's teaching theory, which deemed that the hands, as opposed to the big muscles of the body, played a more significant role in the hitting of the ball.

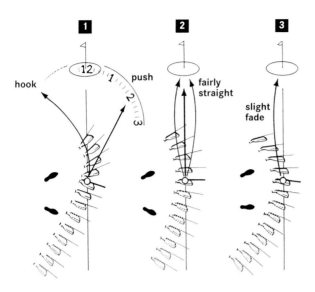

(1) Clubhead moving exaggeratedly from in-to-out; (2) Clubhead moving from in-to-in; (3) Hogan's extreme inside approach to the ball—followed by the club moving sharply inside after impact.

Now, a good player who hits the ball consistently certainly approaches impact on an inside path, but probably not to the extent that Hogan did. It may well feel to that player that the swing is in-to-out somewhat, while the clubhead moves down on its rounded arc to the ball. But think about it. If this were truly an in-to-out swing, the player's divot would look to the right of the target and not squarely at it or a touch left as it did in Hogan's case. The clubhead, in theory, is only on the target line for a few inches at most—in the impact area—and should then swing naturally back to the left or the inside rather than to the right or the outside. The resulting shot pattern will be fairly straight, with not much sidespin attached. Any curvature of the ball will be minimal.

This is especially so these days when the modern golf ball, believe it or not, tends to fly straighter than balls of yesteryear. Players such as Tom Watson and Lee Trevino complain that it's more difficult to shape shots with the modern ball compared to the ball they used when they first came on tour. This, I believe, is one of the reasons there are fewer real shotmakers in the modern game.

Be that as it may, competent golfers need to work the ball from time to time, to fade it or draw it depending on the situation. These golfers shape their shots by varying the degree of the in-to-in path. Additionally, they can adjust their alignment by aiming more left for a bigger fade or right for a larger draw; and they also can manipulate the position of their clubface so that it is either more open or closed at the top of the backswing; or, through impact. It takes practice and educated hands to shape shots, but it's rewarding to be able to pull off a shot that you picture in your mind's eye.

I would like to say this, though. Just as poorer players whose divots look severely left of the target will have difficulty fixing their swings, so too will the true in-to-out swinger whose divots do look to the right of the target. The severe in-to-out shape here is obviously more than a feeling to this player—it does happen. The result is that the hands will have to get quite active to hit the ball on line. It's interesting to note that one of the main reasons for a shank, especially with short irons and pitch shots—and a shank is one of golf's most distressing shots—is that people swing too much in-to-out and catch the ball out on the hosel of the club.

The problem for good golfers, and we'll never know if this was the situation with Hogan early on, is that when they hit a shot to the left, instinct tells them to swing more out to the right, or more in-to-out, to cure that left shot. Unfortunately, the more you swing in-to-out, the more the hands are forced to work through impact, which will, in theory, result in more of a hook as the hands react aggressively to try to square the face—a vicious cycle. If the hands are a little late or slow, the clubface will remain open, producing a push or a block to the right.

In-to-in generally means more body is involved in the release, making the hands more passive; this is the modern way of releasing the club. With an in-to-out type of swing, the player who hits a lot of practice balls and who has educated hands along with rhythm and timing can certainly hit the ball with a fair degree of consistency. But overall, active hands and wrists do not provide the most reliable way of striking the ball with control.

Don't be misled by Hogan's relatively high follow-through position that is apparent in certain photographs; it's clearly more upright than the slot the club occupies at the completion of his backswing. This position does not indicate that Hogan has swung on an in-to-out path, as is the case with many golfers who finish high in order to keep the ball from going left. I believe that Hogan's lateral hip slide is the major cause of his high finish. Let me explain why. The slide toward the target positioned his hips well forward. As his hips began to rotate open from this forward position, Hogan raised his body and stood up on the shot after impact. The club at this stage was swinging well left of his body, but the upward motion of his torso carried his arms and club high up to his famous tall-looking finish. When it came to the longer clubs such as the driver and fairway woods, Hogan's follow-through appeared flatter, but this was an illusion. Having reached the high follow-through position with these clubs, Hogan simply relaxed his arms and just let the club fall into what appeared to be a low, rounded follow-through—but this look was of a position he reached after the fact. It is typical of a fader's follow-through position that he swings left and then up to a high finish.

Hogan did say that the plane shallows on the downswing. I agree, but with a difference. I believe that the golfer who has a slightly steeper plane back and then drops his club onto a shallower plane will be more likely to achieve the correct on-plane look coming down. Hogan's flat backswing plane and dynamic

Hogan's high finish did not mean he swung in-to-out.

change of direction produced the look where his club approached the ball on a path too much below the plane line set up at address—too much, at least, for most golfers. The image Hogan provides of his sheet of glass looking more to the right on the downswing gives the impression that his arms and the club drop inside and behind the line on which he swung them back. This image may be helpful for someone trying to cure a slice but, I believe, would only accentuate a hooker's problem. It was only when Hogan got the clubface wide open that he was able to compensate for his under-plane look coming into the ball, and solve his hooking problem.

I look for the club to be parallel to and fractionally above the shaft plane line coming down, and then on it through impact. I want to refer back to my idea of using the shaft plane at address as a guide to the overall swing plane. I feel that from about halfway down, one should never let any part of the club drop under the original shaft line. If it does, the

Clubhead below plane line indicates club swinging too much from inside.

Clubhead outside hands, parallel and just above the line—a square approach.

clubhead in my view is traveling too much from the inside (approaching on too shallow an angle) and on a track too much from behind the player, in a trapped position—one from which it is constantly difficult to recover, except, of course, in Hogan's case. You can check this on video. First, when examining your address position, draw a line up through the clubshaft and beyond with an erasable marker. Examine the clubhead location from about halfway down to see whether it is below or above the line.

If the club is parallel to and just above the line as it is coming down into impact—as I feel it should—with the butt end of the club swinging to the left, then approaching impact the clubhead will be outside of the hands; the pros refer to this as the club being "out in front of them" as opposed to being "behind them." (Check to see if your shaft matches up to the line at impact.) As a point of reference, the position that the club gets into just before impact should be almost identical to where it was at that stage on the takeaway—the clubhead

is outside the hands in both cases. I really feel that getting into this position approaching impact helps ensure a square, solid hit.

Nick Price, whose ball-striking has been compared to Hogan's, epitomizes this shaft motion—slightly steeper going back, shallower, parallel to and above the plane line coming down until impact, where it returns to the shaft plane line. His shaft plane at impact basically matches the original address angle, with his club never dropping below the plane line.

This isn't to say that you cannot play effectively if any part of your club drops underneath the original plane line coming into the impact zone; Hogan's club did exactly that, before he managed to get the club back on the plane line at impact. But you will require the speed, agility, and ability of a Hogan to get your hands and club swinging aggressively left through the ball to hold the clubface square through impact, as he did. Good players I have taught frequently do have this Hogan

Nick Price

Hogan's shaft plane line at address.

Hogan's under plane approach to the ball.

characteristic, where the clubhead drops well below the plane line coming down, accentuating the in-to-out move. Frequently they hit pushes and hooks, or simply don't make solid contact with their irons. Hogan's under-plane action was even more of a problem for him in his early days as a professional, when his swing was longer and looser. His excessive wrist cock and swing speed exaggerated his shallow, inside approach to the ball. This meant that his timing had to be perfect, otherwise the shallow, inside approach often led to the hooks he despised.

I do have to say, however, that I often see top players who get the shaft steeper than the plane line at impact and whose hands are higher than their original position; they do it consistently, of course, which is obviously the important factor. I often see this set of conditions when a player is hitting—or, should I say, smashing—a driver, trying to sweep the ball off the tee and hit up on it. Typically the spine angle changes slightly—it gets more vertical. These golfers could almost be said to be standing up on the shot as they release and extend their arms through impact. You see this a lot in modern golf because so many players are using forty-five inch drivers, or even longer, and tee the ball up very high. It's much easier to maintain the spine angle with a forty-three inch driver, and it was not long ago that this length was standard. Golf is a power game today and many players really take a lash at the ball. Standing up on it and leaning back is one way to get power, though not always with total control.

I believe it's a good goal to match the shaft at impact to its line at address. This is particularly important with the irons, where the objectives above all are consistency, accuracy, and distance control. This is why I believe that some players who are good drivers of the ball are only average with the irons and pitching clubs.

A cautionary note is advisable here, in that I don't want you to let this discussion of plane and angles on the downswing confuse you.

I'm including it to help you understand what does take place and what should take place. But don't think about these ideas on the course. You cannot physically control what happens at impact, which is a result of all that has transpired before. Of course it's always a good idea when contemplating swing changes to check what happens at impact in your own swing; apart from examining the divot and the ball flight, you would need a high-speed stop-action video, or a sequence photograph, to really see what the club is doing. Everything happens far too quickly for anybody to pick out what happens without this equipment. This is why video is such a useful tool for examining a player's swing.

Many players who try to fix their own swings without consulting slow-motion video can run into trouble because there's often quite a difference between what a player thinks he's doing and what he is doing, which was often the case even with Hogan. As I've stated before, beware of using only instinct and feel when working on your swing.

It is not always necessary, mind you, to be spot-on while hitting the driver as long as you strike it solidly and get good distance, because driving the ball 270 yards into the right or left edge of the fairway does not normally cause problems. But there is less margin for error with the irons, and I maintain that all the great players have been brilliant iron players. This is especially true of Hogan. The one shot that many purists still talk about was Hogan hitting a 210-yard one-iron from the fairway to the final green at Merion during the 1950 U.S. Open. He hit a perfect shot, forty feet left of and beyond the hole. Hogan needed a par on that last hole to get into a playoff for the championship the next day. He got his par and went on to win that U.S. Open. Yes, Hogan was a brilliant iron player.

The irons are the scoring clubs, so precision is vital. The golfer wants to hit the ball an exact distance, and to combine that with pinpoint

Many top players get the shaft steeper at impact than it was at address, especially when using a driver—the hands are higher at impact and the spine angle appears more vertical.

Standing up and leaning back is one way to get power with the driver.

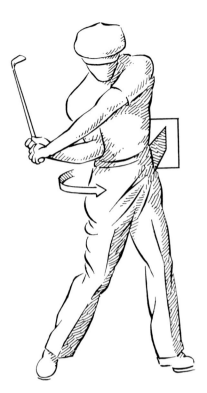

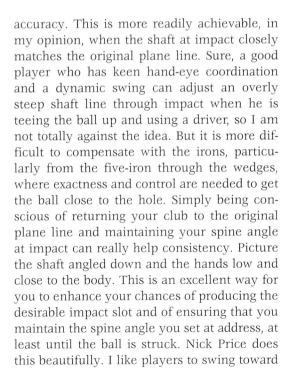

Mirror practice helps develop an understanding of the correct impact position.

Hogan wanted to feel his hips snapping back to the left to start the downswing.

accuracy. This is more readily achievable, in my opinion, when the shaft at impact closely matches the original plane line. Sure, a good player who has keen hand-eye coordination and a dynamic swing can adjust an overly steep shaft line through impact when he is teeing the ball up and using a driver, so I am not totally against the idea. But it is more difficult to compensate with the irons, particularly from the five-iron through the wedges, where exactness and control are needed to get the ball close to the hole. Simply being conscious of returning your club to the original plane line and maintaining your spine angle at impact can really help consistency. Picture the shaft angled down and the hands low and close to the body. This is an excellent way for you to enhance your chances of producing the desirable impact slot and of ensuring that you maintain the spine angle you set at address, at least until the ball is struck. Nick Price does this beautifully. I like players to swing toward

a mirror and pose at impact, then observe and feel this "down-low" position.

Hogan wrote: "The hips initiate the downswing." He emphasized his point by making two pertinent comments: "To begin the downswing turn your hips back to the left," and, "The hips cannot go too fast." I think that these statements have been misinterpreted, and that many golfers have been confused by them over the years. Although Hogan did qualify his assertions by stating that "there must be enough lateral motion forward to transfer the weight to the left foot," I feel that this lateral move has been overlooked, especially when, for example, Hogan in his book provided the image of an elastic strap pulling and spinning the hips left as if he were swinging in a barrel. It's clear on film of Hogan that he had a pronounced lateral move on his downswing before his hips really started to turn to the left.

Hogan's lateral, squatty, sit-down look.

Sam Snead's early sit-down look—less weight transfer to the left side than Hogan.

This move is important to appreciate because Hogan was so emphatic in his advice about turning the hips back to the left to start the downswing. But the millions of golfers who fail to coil correctly on the backswing will run into serious problems when they try to turn their hips as Hogan advised. Turning the hips back to the left would force these players to heave and spin the upper body forward and over, resulting in the club swinging down on a steep plane and an outside-in path. The effect of this motion is that the player will chop down on the ball, producing slices, pulls, weak pop-ups with the driver, and divots looking to the left. This move represents a severe case of what the pros call "coming over the top," and it does not lead to effective golf. Hogan was evidently not conscious of his hip slide toward the target, which in slow-motion film can be seen to take place long before he has completed his backswing. It was a very powerful move in Hogan's case and it gave him a squatty,

sit-down look with his legs. This look is there in so many great ball-strikers. Because of Hogan's big hip slide, his squat appeared different than the one that Sam Snead created. Snead was turned more behind the ball and into his right side at the top of his swing. Therefore Snead did not move as much laterally as he started down—you could say that Hogan's weight transferred to his left side earlier than did Snead's.

Now, Hogan related to his lower body initiating the downswing, which is just about the way every top player has thought of starting back to the ball—his personal key was to turn his hips to initiate the forward movement. I think Jack Nicklaus had it exactly right when he stated, "You start the downswing by unwinding from the ground up." The best players have used many key thoughts related to this statement. Hogan's sequence went like this: he made his initial lateral move, and after his arms started their downward movement, he then

Halfway down, Hogan's hips are still square to the target line.

fully rotated his entire torso at speed—not just his hips but also his upper body—through the ball. Hogan's motion to impact has to be one of the most dynamic, explosive actions ever witnessed. It looks electrifying even in still pictures.

The thought of the whole torso rotating is, I feel, a very good one. Hogan utilized it, as have many fine players. Things happen so quickly on the downswing that it is not possible to tell where the backswing ends and the downswing begins; they are very much a part of each other. I'm sure that Hogan's focus was on his strong glute and hip muscles clearing and opening up quickly to the target. But I feel they got fully into the act much later than he thought; in examining the above illustration you can see that when he is halfway down, his hips are still square or looking at the target line, not open. The action of the lower body is a major key to power and balance in a swing, especially during the change of direction area. Examine the correct movement closely. As you

can see, it involves more than just simply turning the hips to start the downswing, as I will discuss.

In examining many of Hogan's swings prior to and after his accident, I have observed that his swing was definitely shorter and the club-face was more open following his recovery, as I've mentioned in the backswing chapter. I also think that his leg action seemed to quiet down somewhat. The injuries he sustained to his legs may well have kept them from being as active and explosive as they were before his accident. As a result of the combination of his secret, his shorter swing, and calmer leg action, I believe he was able to improve his timing, eliminate the hook and improve on his overall consistency. His tournament results bore this out—his swing was simpler and more efficient. This is just a theory, but I think it has merit. I've seen tremendous improvement in consistency in better players when they learn to develop a calmer, quieter lower body and hip action.

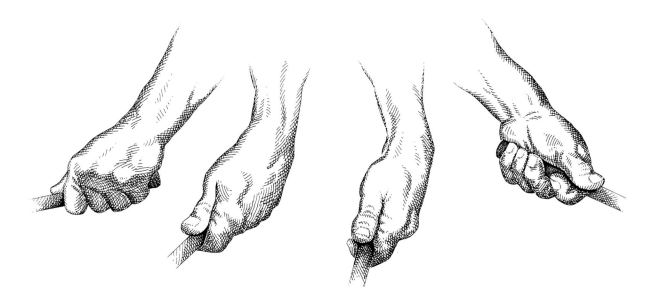

Left wrist supination: palm goes from downward to upward through impact.

Hundreds of swing keys are available to golfers, whatever their abilities; some keys make sense and others are outlandish. Hogan, through his talent and perseverance, found the right keys for him. He talks in depth about supinating the left wrist, where the palm goes from being downward to upward through the impact area so that the wrist bone is raised— the left hand having the appearance of being bowed and arched. He, in effect, thought in terms of the back of the left hand being the clubface, and was then able to control the trajectory and shape of the shot through this supination. Hogan considered trajectory the ultimate criterion in terms of judging how he was hitting the ball. Observers who watched him practice said that they were amazed to see his shots take off on the same arc time after time.

A couple of things to bear in mind regarding supination: it takes quite a bit of practice, and many better golfers who attempt it tend to initially hook or smother the ball. Hogan was able to supinate largely because he had such a "weak" grip (fewer rather than more knuckles showing on the left hand, and the right hand being so much in the fingers). This, along with his famous secret, led in part to the situation in which Hogan came down into the ball with the clubface very open, so much so that observers were sure that the face would never square up; it appeared he could quite conceivably hit a big slice or a shank, so he squared the face up by supinating. But golfers with stronger grips than Hogan's and squarer faces coming down will get the clubface very closed at impact if they try to get into the impact position that he is exaggeratedly posing for in the photo on the next page.

Hogan could be described as an "open-to-closed" player. This defines a player whose clubface is open at the top of the swing (toe pointing downward) and on the way down, then shuts or closes as it approaches impact so as to achieve a square position there. In fact it would probably be closer to the mark to call

Hogan's secret enabled him to have the clubface open approaching impact.

Be aware: if you have a stronger grip than Hogan's and overdo supination, the face will be very closed at impact, resulting in many hooked shots.

Hogan an "open-to-square" player because once he perfected his secret, his club never got closed. Other players are more "closed-to-open." Lee Trevino, who won two U.S. Opens, two British Opens, and two PGA Championships, is one of the finest iron players ever. His clubface was substantially shut or closed at the top (looking more at the sky) and then he worked the clubface open as it approached impact in order for it to be square. Had Trevino supinated his left wrist and rotated his left forearm, as Hogan advised, he would obviously have hit severe low hooks. As it was, he hit one of the greatest controlled fades in the business. And because of his closed position he was able to hit the low, raking shot that was his specialty; no wonder he loved the wind.

Generally, "closed-to-open" players struggle to get some height with their long irons, unless they compensate. They naturally tend to hit them on a low trajectory, as Trevino does.

Some people may say that the "closed-to-open" player has a flaw in his swing, but another way to look at it is as an idiosyncrasy to which the good player must adjust. Trevino struggled at the Augusta National Golf Club in the Masters because there it is vital to maximize distance off the tee—high, right-to-left shots are favored—which means carrying the ball over the course's hills and getting some roll; and it is also helpful there to hit high long-iron shots that will land softly on the firm, very contoured greens. Trevino never did have the trajectory that suited Augusta National, and he knew and accepted this liability. But at the same time he excelled at British Opens, winning back-to-back at Royal Birkdale and Muirfield in 1971 and 1972. Wind is a major element at the British Open. Meanwhile, Trevino was also able to win his two U.S. Opens and two PGA Championships on tough courses; with his wonderful control he was always able to keep the ball in play. His control of the ball suited demanding courses with narrow fairways and penal rough.

There's always a trade-off in golf. Trevino was a strong-willed golfer. He chose to play his way, having developed his technique growing up in the winds of west Texas, and had a brilliant career.

This may be an appropriate time for a digression into golf philosophy. We all need a philosophy if we hope to improve our technique, and the following may give you a clearer picture of how to set out on that course. As I have said, it is practically a physical impossibility for anybody to try to swing exactly like Hogan, or even to create an overall Hoganesque swing look. Hogan's swing evolved to its ultimate details and look as a result of the changes he introduced during his career after sheer hard work, experimentation, and persistence. He was his own laboratory, testing, failing at times, but always keeping his goals in mind. He had a plan, a long-term plan.

Unless you exercise discretion and work in an organized fashion, you may hurt your game if you try to make wholesale swing changes. Always bear in mind that one swing does not fit all, and that you must build your theories and swing keys around your own needs and requirements. That's what Hogan did and it's what every golfer at his or her own level should do.

Here's a possible scenario. Suppose a talented "closed-to-open" player came to me for a lesson. Sure, his clubface is shut at the top, but imagine that he keeps the ball pretty much on line; he hits consistent golf shots. It's possible that this player learned to play under windy conditions or grew up on a tight course where he had to skillfully position his shots. Let's not forget that your swing motion is molded early in your golfing life.

The characteristics a golfer first displays when he takes up the game persist throughout the player's life—be they good or bad. Nick Price has the same tendencies today that can cause him to hit a bad shot—though the tendencies are now somewhat muted—that he had when he was twelve years old, which is when I first saw him swing a golf club. For instance, he still has an overly active leg action sometimes. We continue to work on his tendencies and know they can creep in anytime. Keeping this rule of thumb in mind—that once a tendency, always a tendency—I have to be careful when a student such as the one I described above approaches me for instruction—that naturally "closed-to-open" golfer. How do I proceed when he tells me that he needs help with his long irons because he hits them on a low trajectory without much carry, and so they don't stop when they hit the green? Well, I would suggest some choices: he can think of using a seven-wood (as long as he can handle the damage it might do to his ego), add some loft to the offending clubs, use a softer shaft, or change his technique. Any or all of these ideas might help him solve his problem.

Let's say that we decide to focus on changing this player's technique after discussing his issues and possibly experimenting with other approaches. Now we have to think about how to get his clubface more open at impact so that he will effectively add loft to the club and get the ball up in the air. Should this player make a drastic grip change? This could possibly take a long time to get used to, and there's always the chance that the player will never become comfortable with such a dramatic change. Should he try to open his clubface at the top like Hogan, which may be a tricky proposition? Or do we address his problem from a different angle entirely?

My instincts might tell me that this player could well benefit from adding a simple compensation to his swing so that he can arrive in a more favorable position at impact. Most good players do compensate in one form or another; Hogan certainly did, and he was a great player. The hypothetical player of whom I am speaking probably doesn't have a problem with the middle or shorter irons because they have enough loft, and in fact is likely very accurate with them. He may well have a fairly lofted driver and a lower kick-point in the shaft to get the higher flight and carry he wants with that particular club. I am explaining this in some detail because it is important to understand that going through a swing change is always a process; there's always a certain amount of experimentation along the way to finding the easiest, quickest, and most lasting solution. You cannot just copy verbatim what Hogan said, as sublime a player as he was.

My recommendation for this "closed-to-open" player would be to add in a "cup" to his left wrist so that he could feel it was pronating (knuckles up) as the club works towards impact—exactly what Hogan advised against. This is obviously the antithesis of Hogan's bowing and supinating move. I'm suggesting the fellow could inhibit the counterclockwise rotation of the left forearm on the downswing by sensing that his watch face is looking toward the sky at impact (not that it actually would), providing the hands are still ahead of the clubhead at the point of contact, a position that most good players arrive at. The "cupping" feeling would open the face and add loft, thereby allowing this golfer to release the clubhead. "Holding on" or "hanging on" to the clubhead, as opposed to releasing it, often delofts the clubface, which is exactly what this player does not want to do. Players hold on to the release in order to keep the clubface square or open through impact, in an effort to stop the ball going left. But many times they overdo this non-release and block the shot to the right.

I would certainly try the approach I have recommended for the "closed-to-open" player because he has probably so deeply grooved his move during the course of his golfing life that trying to change things drastically might be too big a shock to his sensory system; it could involve an arduous, time-consuming process for this golfer to ever feel natural with a brand new shape to his swing. Moreover, it could per-

Adding a cup to the left wrist at impact can help certain players.

manently harm his game. Not every golfer—great players included—needs to, should, or does, supinate. You could say that supination was a primary Hogan characteristic. You could also say that better golfers do have their hands ahead of the clubhead at impact, as did Hogan. But the similarity may end there. The fact that the hands are ahead of the clubhead at impact does not mean a player has supinated.

I hope you can now see that Hogan's keys may not be suitable for all golfers. Not every golfer should supinate, or for that matter turn the left hip back to start the downswing. Every golfer needs to be careful about what he takes from his reading of Hogan, or anybody. It is important to sift through the vast amount of information available so that you can discover what works best for you. Be discerning. Be discriminating. Use what you feel applies to your situation and discard the rest. Try something, and work at it deliberately. Be patient and enjoy your experimentation, because this is all part of the search and the journey. Be your own master, however, and let the strike and the ball flight be your ultimate guides. Let them tell you whether you need to change.

In my own studies I have examined Hogan's hand action just after impact on a full shot. His left hand quickly went from a position of being bowed and supinated at the point of

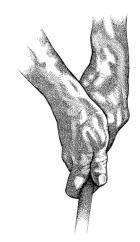

Left hand bowed and supinated at impact.

Cup at the base of the left wrist just past impact.

impact to one where a "cup" formed at the base of the left wrist as the right hand and arm released just after impact. This is evident in his left wrist at the completion of the follow-through, where his arms look relaxed and the "cup" in his left wrist matches the look of the "cup" in the right wrist. Given Hogan's speed, even he with his weak grip would have found it virtually impossible to preserve the supinated look (i.e., the bowed look) for any period after impact without hitting severe hooks; to do so would entail curtailing the use of his right arm and hand through impact, which he didn't want. Hogan had the face open just before impact, then he supinated. This supinating move squared the face at impact and almost simultaneously—as the ball was struck—Hogan added the little cup into his left wrist. In my view this move protected Hogan from oversupinating and closing the face down too much. This ensured that the ball left the clubface squarely and on a good trajectory. Hogan felt that his hands never crossed over; but in fact they did, although well after the ball had been struck. He felt that his right hand worked under his left, which you can see as he really exaggerates the feeling in the photograph on page ninety-six.

When you think about it, Hogan did more than a little manipulating of the clubface in the hitting area. But he had such a sensitive

At the finish, the cup in the left wrist matches the cup in the right wrist.

Hogan did not want his hands to cross over as he demonstrates here.

Hogan wanted the feeling of his right hand under the left.

feel and awareness of his hands that I am convinced his move through impact became a pure reaction, instinctive all the way. He grooved this move, one of the many peerless results he got from all the balls he hit.

One further point regarding supination: It is easier and more desirable to supinate with the irons, where in order to take a divot it is crucial that you make a slight descending blow. However, as a general rule, when using the driver it is preferable to imagine fully releasing the clubhead; the reasons are simply that you want to sweep the ball off the tee and not take a divot with a driver. Imagine that in the impact zone the top of the grip almost points backward, toward the navel rather than leading the clubhead all the way through as with an iron. In other words, the clubhead is being released and encouraged to swing past the

hands as you try to hit the ball slightly on the upswing. This happened even with Hogan to some degree and can be seen in the photograph of him on the next page.

In *Five Lessons* Hogan makes a very interesting statement about the hands, a comment to which I referred earlier in this chapter. "As far as applying power goes I wish that I had three right hands," he writes. His natural left-handedness enabled him to support the club through impact, and his open clubface coming into impact allowed him to hit as aggressively as possible with the right hand without fear of it taking over. Although Hogan may have felt it was his right hand, he was actually using his whole right side, and maybe the statement should have been "three right sides." Not only was his right hand involved with hitting the ball, but so were his right foot, knee, hip, arm,

Hogan demonstrating his ideal impact position with a driver.

Make practice swings and even hit balls with your right hand only to get the feel for how the right side works through impact.

Hogan's strong right side move through the ball was obvious.

and shoulder. This is a great thought, and for players in a good position halfway down, the right side should play a major role in the hit—just like throwing a ball, as Hogan describes.

**I like golfers to make practice swings and even hit balls with the right hand only to get the feel for the right side. Nick Price, like Hogan, is a natural left-hander, and his game really benefited when he learned to hit balls with his less dominant side. Try it yourself with a nine-iron, initially, hitting off tees. In a short space of time, you'll be amazed at the good feelings that you begin to sense, and you'll realize that your right side really does have a big role to play in hitting the ball.**

Now let's look at the lower body once again, this time through impact. Hogan describes the correct leg action as that in which the left knee bows out and the weight moves to the outside of the left foot. (These thoughts are in keeping with a strong lateral move of the legs, as Hogan had.) I firmly believe that at impact

A braced left leg just past impact: a superb image to copy.

the left leg is not totally locked, but should be straightening as it receives the full force of the hit. It has to resist as the arms and the club fly by; many better players over the years have thought about a braced left leg through impact, and I believe players should apply this thought today. Keeping the left leg too bent, in my opinion, doesn't supply the necessary resistance. Hogan in action did bow his left knee to some degree coming into the ball, but I'm sure that in the impact area it straightened earlier than he felt; his foot seems very well planted with only a little weight to its outside. It really is an unbelievably powerful, dynamic position, and offers a superb image for golfers to copy.

Finally, Hogan's awareness of how the laws of physics generated a multiplying factor in the swing to produce power was extraordinary. He applied the laws to his own swing. His speed and power were phenomenal, and the photograph on the next page of him in full flow captures the essence of what made him such a fabulous ball-striker. His insight that speed multiplies the golfer's power in a chain reaction from the hips through the shoulders to the arms and hands, and finally to the clubhead, is almost identical to what modern sport scientists are discovering. Examine the accompanying graph that analyzes the way energy is transferred in an efficient swing. The transfer

Ben Hogan in full flow: speed, power, balance, athleticism.

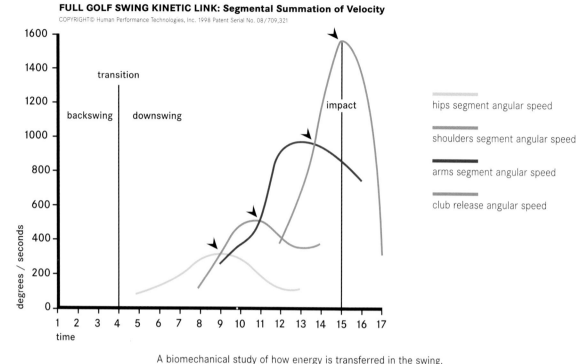

**FULL GOLF SWING KINETIC LINK: Segmental Summation of Velocity**

COPYRIGHT© Human Performance Technologies, Inc. 1998 Patent Serial No. 08/709,321

hips segment angular speed

shoulders segment angular speed

arms segment angular speed

club release angular speed

A biomechanical study of how energy is transferred in the swing.

occurs in the following manner: the hips slow down prior to impact, passing the energy to the shoulders. The shoulders then slow down, passing the energy to the arms and hands. The arms and hands then slow down just prior to impact, passing the energy to the clubhead, and then into the ball. This efficient movement cannot be detected with the naked eye, and can only be quantified with digital computer analysis. You can see that as the one graph peaks, the energy is then transferred to the next component. Good technique means building an efficient swing, which derives from an efficient transfer of energy resulting in maximum power through impact. Apart from video, I am now using biomechanical analysis in my teaching to help analyze golfers and to help improve their swing efficiency. We are seeing startling increases in power and consistency, and I'm sure such analysis will be part of golf instruction in the new millennium. Although it sounds complex, it makes learning easier, because it's all about developing

motion as opposed to just thinking of static positions in the swing, something of which we are all guilty at times. Hogan epitomizes efficiency in a golf swing. I like the term "proper sequential motion," or quite simply, superb timing of all the components producing that "sweet feeling" of solid contact.

## To Become an 80-Breaker—or Better

I have always believed that when building a solid swing one has to be aware of the various components involved and how they interact. Obviously, once you have established a good, solid setup (grip and posture), the two major components remaining are the body and that of the arms and hands. By working on them separately and then putting them together, you can achieve a comprehensive understanding of the parts and the whole.

The lower body has to move first in the downswing. I've indicated that Hogan stressed that for him this meant thinking of turning his hips. It

This drill will train you to make the correct transition from backswing to downswing.

is essential, if the chain reaction is to operate in the correct sequence, that the lower body does move first—I cannot overemphasize this.

**Consider the drill we mentioned in the last chapter where you fold your arms across your midsection. Get into a good posture and make the backswing motion. Make a full turn, sensing the stability in the lower body as you wind up. Be aware of your stomach muscles tightening. As you are completing the motion back, and moving into your right side, start the motion forward simultaneously by a lateral move of the left knee toward the target, followed fractionally thereafter by the left hip. Feel some weight moving to the front of the left foot, and most importantly, feel pressure going down from the left foot into the ground. Almost at the exact same time you should then feel pressure and weight going down through the right foot into**

**the ground. I call this sensation "being grounded." It is a strong move in which you are pushing your lower body down into the ground and using the ground to enhance your resistance and stability. The weight distribution at this stage feels about 50/50 between the left foot and the right foot.**

Many players go wrong in that they feel no downward pressure and try to slide too much weight over to the left side too early. The legs, and, more vitally, the ground, do not then provide the stability or resistance necessary to create speed or generate consistency on the downswing; in other words, an inefficient transfer of energy results. Compensations for this slide will then have to be made coming into impact; one such compensation occurs when a player hangs and tilts back with the upper body in order to allow the hands and arms to catch up. This applies especially to junior players, whose hips and legs, being proportionally stronger than the rest of their body, move in an overly aggressive and uncontrolled manner. The result is that these juniors are almost airborne at impact. This excessive leg action can remain with a golfer throughout his life. It is important to learn the correct lower body action, for power, balance, and stability.

The feeling of turning back away from the target while you're moving the lower body (left knee) toward the target is crucial if you plan to develop a dynamic swing. This powerful move loads up, bends, and energizes the shaft as it changes direction. Golfers are often not aware of this double-directional move, but to varying degrees it is definitely there in the transition. The move was most apparent in Hogan's swing.

A golf swing is not really a backswing and a downswing as such. We use these terms to help analyze the motion in stop-action film. Rather, the swing is a continuous motion during which the upper body is turning away from the target for a fraction of a second while the lower body is at the same time just beginning to unwind toward it. This dynamic action builds up an impressive amount of leverage in the swing. Practice this change of direction move using the arms-folded exercise; wind and stretch going back and then start to unwind, making only a short initial move forward. Hold this dynamic transition position for a few seconds and then repeat. Do this a few times and recall your feelings. Allow yourself to move a little laterally as you make the transition; feel that your left knee and hip are moving toward the target, even that they are moving to the right of the target.

You might wonder: What about the weight transfer to the left? This does occur, but it should be subtle and in conjunction with the slight lateral move forward. If you go overboard in thinking about weight transfer it's easy to slide your body too far forward, thereby compromising your stability and getting out of

Moving forward while coiling back: a dynamic swing results.

synch with your arm motion. In my opinion, Hogan was the exception rather than the rule in terms of the extent of his lateral slide. He only got away with what could technically be called a fault because of the exceptional speed of his hands and arms. This speed allowed his hands and arms to catch up to his body.

I'd like you to really sense the "groundedness" you have created. Sense pressure being built up through your feet bearing down on the ground. This vital "sit-down" move, or bracing of the legs, provides balance and resistance; it adds further leverage to the swing. Focus on these elements in the drill to become familiar with the sensations.

A particularly poetic and apt observation that I once read about Hogan was that "he had a wonderful liaison with the turf." What an

After the transition, rotate the torso fast to the finish.

image! Hogan felt this contact with the turf was so important that he insisted an extra spike be placed in his right shoe under the ball of his foot. He later took this idea further when he added an extra, or thirteenth, spike, to his left shoe. Hogan was interested in every detail that could help him improve. He wanted to be connected to the ground, to feel rooted. In such small details we find the measure of this deeply interesting man.

**Let's carry on with the arms-folded drill. During the transition forward, I'd like you to retain or even increase the feeling of tightness in your stomach area that you felt on the backswing. Having grounded yourself via a slight lateral move, you are now in position to complete the "clearing" action of your torso. The hips can rotate fast all the way to the finish from here; I**

**am using the word "rotate" but you can also think of this move as spinning, clearing, or opening the hips. The central consideration is that it is from here that you accelerate and pour on the power through impact. Allow your right knee to kick in so that at the finish you are balanced on your left foot and right toes, knees touching, right shoulder looking at the target. Remain aware of your "grounding" coming into the impact area. Try to keep your right foot on the turf as long as possible, until your rotating body pulls it off the ground. Hogan did this so well, especially with his middle and short irons. The longer you keep your right foot on the ground through impact the more likely it is that you will retain your spine angle there. Golfers whose legs are too active often lose their spine angle.**

Hogan kept his right foot down as long as possible.

The golfer who maintains through impact the spine angle and posture he formed at address will have gone a long way toward creating consistency, most particularly with the irons. To reiterate, maintaining spine angle is a major factor in allowing the golfer to return the club into a repetitive "slot" at impact.

The concept of the stomach muscles being tightened is an important one. In many of the martial arts your power, force, and speed come from your core or center, which is located around your navel. A useful image is that of tightening both ends of a wet towel and wringing it continuously so the middle gets squeezed dry. Relate that to the upper and lower parts of your body as you wind back and tighten your stomach muscles; now you are ready to unwind coming back down. Practice the arms-folded exercise often to instinctively build up the feel for how the body works going back, into the transition, through the impact area

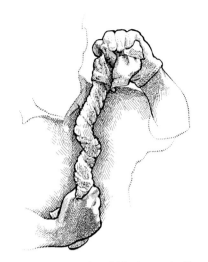

Wringing a towel to squeeze the middle dry can be likened to tightening the stomach muscles during the swing.

Complete shoulder turn, short arm swing.

and on to the finish.

Another major benefit of moving in two directions at once—going back as you're going forward—is that this will tend to shorten the swing. As you start the movement forward, the arms cannot travel that much further back. Shortening the distance that the arms travel back simplifies and synchronizes the swing as long as turn is not sacrificed. The shorter the distance the arms have to travel, the easier it is to get them in the correct position coming down. *The ideal combination is a complete shoulder turn allied to a short arm swing with a relatively full wrist cock.* This shorter version not only improves consistency, accuracy, and control, but it will also increase power. This compact position, linked to a dynamic change of direction, encourages an increase in the wrist cock as the club moves down. This "downcocking" action, as it is called, adds leverage to the swing and increases "snap" and speed through impact. Tiger Woods is the perfect example of somebody who produces explosive power from a compact swing. Nobody hits the ball harder in the modern game.

Now let's move on to the other component of the downswing: the motion of the hands and arms. First, consider the movement of the right arm; its motion is one of the key areas in the downswing. As the downswing starts, the right elbow drops downward toward the right hip, while the hands maintain their distance from the chest; another way to look at this is that the hands maintain their width from the chest. This dynamic look is not unlike that of an archer pulling an arrow from his quiver as he prepares to load his bow. There's no wasted motion; it's simply a matter of transferring the top of the backswing position down.

Hogan's image of a sidearm throwing motion will help you understand the motion of the right arm. As in the throwing motion, the right elbow leads the arm and is in a bent formation under the left elbow; this ensures that the clubhead lags behind the hands.

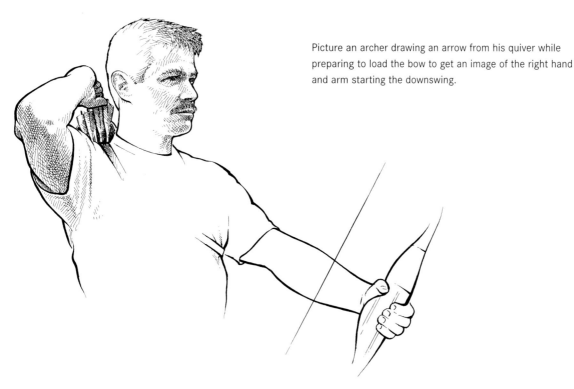

Picture an archer drawing an arrow from his quiver while preparing to load the bow to get an image of the right hand and arm starting the downswing.

Again, here we have that path which all solid ball-strikers take back to the ball—an inside path along with a fairly shallow plane. Many high-handicap amateurs have their right elbow positioned above the left and well away from the hip. This creates a steep angle and an early weak release into the ball along an out-side-in path. **To build up a feel for this area of the swing, it's helpful to swing down and pose in the correct pre-impact position, where the right elbow is adjacent to and in front of the right hip. Hold this position for a few seconds, as illustrated at right, and then swing aggressively to the finish. Build the muscle memory, for if you can arrive in this position it makes impact, the next link in the chain, easier to reach. Now you are in a power position from which you can definitely deliver the clubhead to the ball using the "three right hands" that Hogan says he wishes he had.**

Pose in this pre-impact position for a few seconds before swinging to the finish.

The right arm action on the downswing is similar to a sidearm throwing motion.

An exercise Hogan advocates, and which may help confirm the proper feelings with your arms and hands, consists of your taking a basketball or soccer ball or, even better, a light medicine ball, and tossing it at a specific spot on a wall, or to a partner. Release the ball at the same angle that you would a golf club. You go through the same swing motion as if you were hitting a ball, though the movement back will be fairly restricted because of the ball being positioned in your hands. You must feel the two-directional move, the grounding, and the stomach muscles, as I have described. As you release the ball with full velocity to a set target, sense that as you unwind the body you fling the arms and hands, allowing the left arm to fold as you swing through; this is what should happen during your actual swing. You should feel that your hands and arms rush by your body through impact. Many players have expressed a key thought to me in this regard, as follows: they feel that their arms, hands, and club pull their body through to the finish, which is an ideal sensation for those high-handicap golfers who overuse their bodies on the downswing. Be aware when you work on your dynamic body motion that you always keep your arms relaxed—no death grip.

Let's now touch once again on the supination theory. In the impact area, Hogan really emphasized supination—which, to remind you, occurs as the left hand gradually rotates from a palm-down position near the top of the swing and works toward a palm-up position coming into impact. To use another image, supination is the face of your watch going from looking toward the sky to looking in the direction of the ground. As you know, I've referred frequently in this chapter to supination in a variety of contexts; it was an essential element in Hogan's swing theory. In fact, it's difficult to think about Hogan's swing without reflecting on supination. Now, the only danger in turning the left hand down or rotating the knuckles to the ground is that the clubface can close severely. Generally, as long as a person's

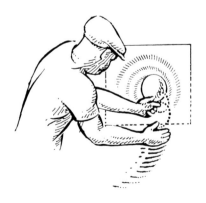

Throwing a ball to a target gives one an awareness of the motion of the arms and hands during the swing.

grip is neutral, I agree with the concept of supination, especially as long as it is not overdone. Supination can also be beneficial when you are hitting shots into the wind, because then you are seeking a piercing trajectory. But as I said earlier, extreme supination can cause problems. You must take your own situation into account.

While supination is more a move for the better player, I also like it for less-accomplished golfers who tend to hit fat or thin iron shots, or whose ball flight has no penetration as a result of an open or scoopy clubface making contact with the ball. These players, as Hogan said earlier, get their hands behind the clubhead at impact, often resulting in a glancing blow and a weak hit. Supination will encourage the face to close through the ball, ensuring a more powerful square-face hit. It can help players who hit weak fades or slices, enabling them to hit solid draws. Rather than getting too technical with higher handicappers, I try to limit them to the simple image of the watch face looking toward the ground at impact. If this is going to occur, the left forearm and wrist must rotate down in a counterclockwise motion, which helps the clubface close. To get the feel of this, practice making smooth half-swings holding the club with your left hand alone and swinging waist-high to waist-high. Focus on the face of your watch, trying to feel it going from looking at the sky from the top of your swing to looking toward the ground through impact. This is the key feeling to maintain here; of course, though, your watch face cannot actually point to the ground at impact, but I am offering this image because I want you to accentuate the feel of supination. If the ball starts going to the left, then you're overdoing it.

A few words of advice for those better players wishing to experiment with supination: I have found that the problems associated with supination lie normally not in the left hand but more often with the dominant right hand.

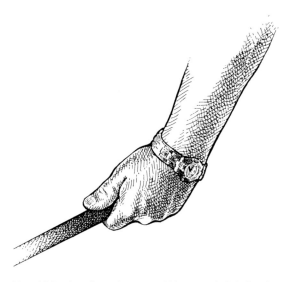

Many higher-handicap players would improve their ball-striking if they tried to get the watch face on their left hand looking toward the ground at impact.

The problem is that the right hand and forearm roll excessively as they approach the ball, which shuts or closes the clubface prior to impact. Deep divots and smothered pull hooks result. As I said in the middle section of this chapter, Hogan never felt his hands cross over. To further your understanding of supination, hit some three-quarter wedge shots, trying to keep them on a low trajectory. You can facilitate this low trajectory by placing the ball a bit further back in your stance. As you supinate your left hand gradually through impact, make sure you focus also on the right hand; pay particular attention to the trigger (index) finger, concentrating on the knuckle to control and

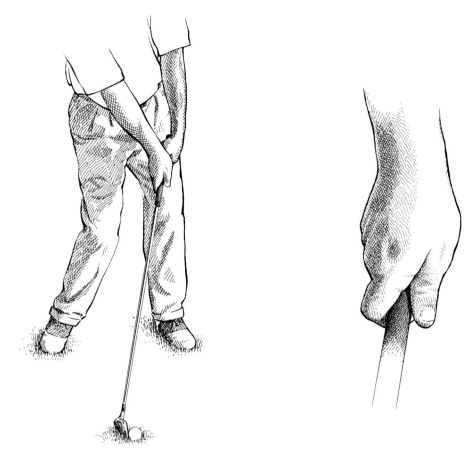

Excessive rolling of the right hand and forearm closes the face prior to impact, and will ruin supination of the left hand.

support the shaft in order to maintain a square to slightly open clubface approaching impact. The sensation you want at impact (and that I find works well for many players) should be that the pad above the right thumb and the fingernails on your right hand point more toward the sky than to the ground, and that your right hand also feels "under" the left hand and not on top of it. This is where blending feelings and mechanics is really important; it's like getting the right mix of ingredients into a cake. Some players might have to focus on more left-hand supination, while others might have to work on adding some right-hand-under feeling. There's no way to get away from the fact that some experimentation and trial and error is involved in golf. Fiddling around with feelings is what often leads to that "I've got it" statement.

The net result of the correct hand position through impact is that the clubface should contact the ball with the heel leading the toe slightly. The right hand, as opposed to rolling excessively, should now be in a more neutral position. At impact the right hand should show a slight "cup" at the base of the wrist, helping to ensure that the clubface doesn't close prematurely.

Your wedge shots should now be a lot lower; if you have struck the ball crisply then the ball will sit down quickly on the green. So, to supinate correctly, allow the left hand to rotate down, and the right hand to hold the face square or open. This takes some practice, but on the whole the golfer who is able to supinate will, as Hogan states, learn to deloft and control the clubface

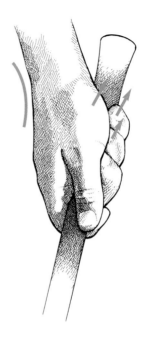

The role of the right hand as the left hand supinates: knuckle on the trigger finger helps support shaft and control clubface; fingernails and pad above thumb point to the sky; slight cup at base of wrist.

through impact. This will produce divots that are wide, shallow, and uniform, and that pleasing result: perfectly flighted iron shots.

A closing thought on the downswing: There's no question about whether impact is the most important position in the swing. Of course it is. However, it is a position within a motion and is but the culmination of what has transpired before. Having an awareness of where you should be at impact and also at the finish can really help in building a swing and providing a goal that you can work toward.

**To this end, I suggest this two-part drill. First, with the aid of a mirror opposite you, and looking at yourself face-on, adopt a perfect impact position (and Hogan wouldn't be a bad person to copy). Hogan's impact position looked like this: hands ahead of the clubhead; left arm extended and linked to the chest; right arm bent; right elbow adjacent to the right hip and the inner part of the elbow pointing to the sky; head behind the ball; right shoulder set lower than the left; right knee and right foot working inward toward the target; left leg braced, supporting the transfer of weight.**

**Hold this position and repeat it a few times. Once you have attained a feeling of where you should be at impact, go to the range and move into the second phase of the drill. With the ball now in front of you, again assume your impact position. Once again, remain in this spot for a few seconds, making it as dynamic as possible. Push the clubhead into the ground if necessary.**

**Then, starting from this modified address, pause a couple of seconds, make your backswing, and then hit the ball. It might take you a few shots to get your timing right but it won't be long before you're hitting them solidly. Upon reverting to your normal address poition, try to recreate the same impact sensations during your actual swing on the way to the finish.**

As far as the finish is concerned, you can't go wrong in mimicking certain aspects of Hogan's position (right): the left leg supporting the weight of the body; the right foot poised up on the toes; hips fully cleared; right shoulder pointing to the target; hands finishing well left of the torso; right arm fully extended and folded; left arm beautifully supporting the club; eyes following the flight of the ball. Note also Hogan's effortless torso position—his signature, really—in which he finishes almost straight up and down with no pressure on the lower back. Here you have a classic, balanced finish to a classic swing. Ben Hogan looked like he could hit a shot and hold his finish for eternity.

Hogan's impact position.

# SUMMARY & CONCLUDING THOUGHTS

Ben Hogan's golfing philosophy was built around his uncovering and incorporating a few fundamentals into his swing. After years of study and experimentation, Hogan identified those few fundamentals and felt that their presence in his swing guaranteed good form, which for Hogan meant a swing that provided power, accuracy, control over the golf ball and, most of all, consistency. Having stripped his swing down to these fundamentals, Hogan stayed with them. He did not try to perfect every detail of the swing, and it was only when he found what he needed that his game reached a new level. As he writes, "I honestly began to feel that I could count on playing fairly well each time I went out, that there was no practical reason for me to feel I might

suddenly 'lose it all.' I would guess that what lay behind my new confidence was this: I had stopped trying to do a great many difficult things perfectly because it had become clear in my mind that this ambitious overthoroughness was neither possible nor advisable, or even necessary. All you needed to groove were the fundamental movements—and there weren't so many of them."

Of course it can take a serious commitment of study and time to groove the fundamental movements, and also an appreciation for a tremendous level of detail. I've provided a substantial amount of detail in this book, but by no means do I want you to suffer from paralysis by analysis. That's the furthest thing from my mind as a teacher. I constantly remind players to work on details only on the practice tee, or even without a ball at home, where there's no pressure to hit good shots. Practicing and playing are entirely different worlds. You practice and work on things so that you can groove them into your swing, so that you can then go out on the golf course and play through instinct. You work on details in order to incorporate them and make them part of you. To help my students learn the details so that they can later incorporate them instinctively, it is crucial that as a teacher I understand their learning styles. Players differ widely in their ability and willingness to handle in-depth details of technique. Some players are analytical while others find it difficult to think about technique, so I have to approach each player in a slightly different manner.

I can provide an example of this in Seve Ballesteros, with whom I worked in 1991. No golfer is more of a feel player than Seve, and when he asked me to work with him I was very conscious of the fact that I had to keep things simple and communicate my thoughts in a feel mode. We basically worked on two elements the whole year—making his posture more athletic and tightening up his turn to create more consistency. We worked on these two aspects the entire year, and to my way of

thinking they worked well inasmuch as he kept the ball more in play and was the leading money-winner in Europe that year. However, although he started off well the following year, it wasn't long before he came to me and said, "David, thanks for the help but the ideas we worked on last year were too technical and I need to go back to feel." In retrospect, this may not have been the best solution for him. But a player has to decide which road he wants to take. I mention this example because it shows that every player is different as far as the learning curve is concerned.

If you wish to change your technique you need to blend mechanics and feel, and you must be able to switch from working on mechanics during practice to playing by feel on the course (especially in rounds that count, as opposed to those in which you are practicing and, perhaps, working on technique). The moral of the story is that you should work on only one or two thoughts or keys at a time. More does not mean better. Take an idea or two out to the range and limit yourself to working on those aspects only. Once you feel you have assimilated the ideas, then you can work on the next ideas. Always remember that the swing is a linked action, and that it's important to work on the basics, starting from the grip and then working through the swing. Remember that what you work on initially will influence what occurs later. Hogan always practiced with a reason and purpose in mind. So should any golfer.

I would like to make a couple of other points. The exciting thing about studying Hogan and learning about the swing—I continue to learn about it every day—is that it becomes a lifelong hobby. Hogan provided many insights, but he also implied a great deal and left plenty of room for interpretation. Following are a few other thoughts on the swing that are worth examining.

**Tempo**

Hogan told one of his ardent admirers, Gary

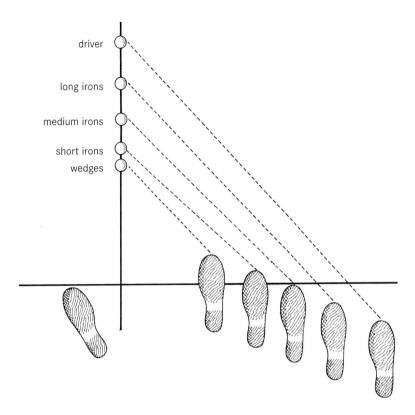

Hogan's ball position theory: ball stays in same place while stance width varies. Feet get closer together and aimed more open (left) as club gets shorter.

Player, that if one's swing were fundamentally sound, then good tempo would follow naturally. There was no need to think of it. Hitting as many balls as Hogan did, though, he always knew if his tempo was off. I like players to make practice swings with their eyes closed. It helps them to get less mechanical and to feel the tempo of their swings. You might want to try this.

**Ball Position**

Hogan liked to position the ball approximately one-half inch to an inch inside his left heel no matter what club he was using. He felt the fundamental swing was the same whatever club he was using, so there was no reason ball position should vary. He varied only the width of his stance. For the short irons—six-iron through the wedge—the stance became nar-rower and more open as the clubs got shorter, his right foot moving progressively closer to the left foot and toward the ball/target line. This position in effect shortens the swing with these clubs because it restricts the turn, even though you feel you are actually making a full swing. It also gives the player the freedom to easily clear the left hip out of the way on the downswing because it is now pulled back, or pre-cleared, one might say. Hogan's belief was that this stance might cost a bit of distance with the short irons, but will certainly add to one's accuracy. For longer clubs, Hogan advocates a wider stance for balance and stability in which the right foot is pulled back in a slightly closed position. Although Hogan did say, as indicated above, that the fundamental swing remains the same from club to club, he added that subtle changes occur without the

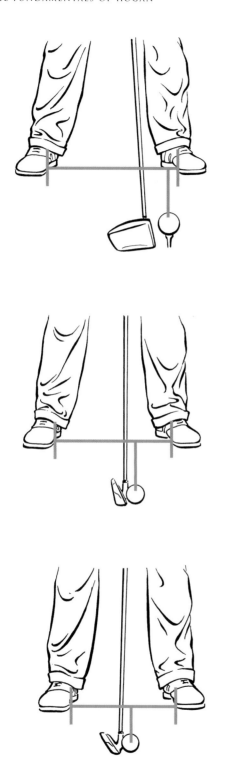

Another way to think about ball position; move the ball back as you go from driver through mid-irons to short-irons.

player being conscious of these variations. The longer the club, the flatter the lie angle, the farther you stand from the ball. This naturally produces a slightly flatter plane. The opposite is true for the shorter clubs, which leads to a slightly more upright plane. Obviously, the swing with the wedge is more upright than the swing with a three-iron.

I must stress that these changes to the plane should occur naturally and without your thinking about them, and that they are almost imperceptible to the naked eye; the design of the club makes the changes happen. However, I would ask you to experiment in the area of ball position, and suggest this alternative. Try three varying ball positions for all your clubs: (1) well forward in the stance, close to the left heel for the sweeping driver and fairway wood swing; (2) two balls back of the driver position for the mid- and long-irons; and (3) approximately in the middle of the stance for the short irons. Adopt a slightly wider stance for the longer clubs as well, and a narrower one for the shorter irons. I have found this to be a simple but very effective approach for weekend players, but even many tour players utilize this method as it does offer a little leeway for variation. My preference would be to move the ball around a bit. On the one hand, you might think that Hogan's way would at first glance be easier to repeat, and this would be true under constant playing conditions. However, golf is such a feel game that one has to deal with many varying situations: different slopes, low and high shots, draws, fades, three-quarter shots, wind, and all the other possibilities inherent in an outdoor game played on courses of varying dimensions and topography. I am certain the reason many accomplished players move the ball around is because they know you can't play the game without some feel. The point is that instinct plays a large role in a golfer finding the proper ball location. And so one cannot and should not be robotic in this area because the golf course with all the situations that require a variety of shots, differs from the perfect setting of the practice tee.

Although Ben Hogan advised one ball position for all clubs, he did alter it at times, as can be seen above with a wedge, showing that he was as much a feel player as a mechanical player.

It is noticeable in the photograph of Hogan addressing the ball with a lofted wedge that he himself has positioned the ball farther back in his stance than he advocates. Although he would certainly be considered a mechanical player, I believe he relied on feel as well. He was always shaping the shots and doing something with the ball to fit the look of the hole. I'm sure, then, that whether consciously or otherwise, he at times changed his ball location, especially with the shorter irons. My advice is to experiment; find what works best for you. You can also apply a general rule: play the ball more forward in your stance if you tend to hook or push your shots. Bring the ball back if you tend to slice or pull.

But whatever approach you choose, be consistent. When I ask a new pupil what he would like to have happen in his golf game, he invariably replies, "To be more consistent." Consistency starts at address. And ball position plays a significant part in consistency.

So do athleticism, rhythm, and power, factors every golfer should always be looking to incorporate into his game. Hogan's swing, whether observed in full motion, stop-action photography, or in an artist's rendering, embodied those qualities. An economy of movement made his swing a blend of both art and science; it functioned beautifully as well as efficiently.

"As you work on the details, keep in mind that you are indeed grooving the fundamentals—the goal," Hogan said. For Hogan, grooving the fundamentals meant he could focus on managing his game and scoring. His fundamentals became part of him, signatures of his golfing personality. The keynotes, or fundamentals, for him, consisted of his being properly positioned at address with the correct stance and grip; waggling the club in a way that prepared him for the upcoming shot; starting back with his hands, arms, and shoulders, in that order, which in turn would pull the hips around; staying on plane; initiating the downswing by turning the hips; supinating the left wrist and hitting through the shot to a balanced finish; and, of course, he added his personal "secret." I hope this book has provided you with the information to develop your own keys. The lesson you can learn from Hogan is that once you have refined your keys, persevere and stick to them.

Hogan's view of the swing, which he gained only after years of enjoyably hard work, sounds simple enough. He did manage to boil down his extensive studies to provide a road map which he believed would guide the golfer committed to the journey toward long-term and steady improvement. The written word isn't always the easiest medium by which to communicate golf instruction. Hogan's teachings, and, I hope, this text, along with the photographs and illustrations, will simplify your task of understanding and learning the key swing movements, along with providing you some choices and alternatives. I have tried to make this approach as clear and succinct as possible, all the while realizing that it is very easy for people to misinterpret written instruction. When I'm working one-on-one

with a person, I always have the chance to rephrase an idea for that particular person. In a book you only have one shot at it, and you are addressing a larger audience, not an individual. Keeping this in mind, I have tried to provide not only some alternative ways of looking at the golf swing, but also some ways for you to think about the swing. My overriding intention—the one theme I've tried to keep clear in my own mind—is to help you improve your own game. I suggest that if you have now read this book in its entirety, you go back and reread chapters one through four. Work on each chapter until you feel you have assimilated its information. Then go on to the next chapter and do the same until you have completed this process with each chapter. You are following Hogan's philosophy of building a swing brick by brick. The beauty of this method is that you can consider the material a constant source of reference to which you can return as you improve.

We have learned a great deal about what really happens in the swing since Hogan's most influential work, *Five Lessons,* was published in 1957, as he knew we would. As popular as Hogan's book has been, I have found that many golfers have had a difficult time incorporating all of his ideas in ways that could help them. Loyal Hogan followers who were in awe of his impressive, almost immaculate game, felt that they too could find such near-perfection by adopting his teachings in *Five Lessons.* Hogan did not want golfers to copy his every move, and in fact wrote that players who used his book would nevertheless adopt different looks; that's just human nature. But at the same time he did say that all good golfers share common traits. Many golfers who use *Five Lessons,* though, have tried to copy his moves to the nth degree; they read his book as if that's what he wanted them to do. They tried to reproduce his swing by adopting his weak grip, which for most golfers reduces power. They tied their arms together and kept them stuck so close together throughout the swing that they appeared wrapped in a wet suit, but their swings looked tight and lacked rhythm, and I've often wondered how they could feel any freedom of motion. These golfers worked painfully hard to get the club on a Hogan-type plane, many swinging too flat in the process, and then snapped their hips around to start their downswings. In my view many people became frustrated when they chose to follow Hogan's advice slavishly, without taking into account their idiosyncrasies. At the same time, one of the most valuable contributions that Hogan made through his book is that he sparked debate and discussion. That debate continues.

*Five Lessons* included such difficult concepts as plane, pronation, and supination. Many of Hogan's followers, who through no fault of their own had neither the natural talent nor physical capabilities of an athlete, much less of the master himself, and who may not have had the time to practice for hours every day as he loved to do, became discouraged. Their discouragement was quite natural, since golfers have always felt drawn to the idea that a magic answer or tip would instantly resolve their problems and turn them into better players. But Hogan's book did not provide a shortcut to improvement, nor did he intend it to. It demanded thorough, hard work, and copious amounts of patience.

*Five Lessons* and all of Hogan's writings were optimistic. He conveyed so clearly his belief that golfers willing to commit themselves to change could improve. Like Hogan, I also believe we can improve. I also believe wholeheartedly that there is no single approach as far as improvement is concerned, and that a golfer must always take into account his or her talent level, desire, goals, time commitment to practice and play, physical conditioning and age in the equation. Following a formula does not guarantee improvement. On the other hand, following guidelines within which you can improvise and experiment and come up with your own answers can very often lead to lasting improvement.

It is unfortunate that so many Hogan disciples became confused. Many of them erred in believing there was something wrong with them when they could not copy Hogan's swing, rather than realizing it was impossible, given the differences between them and Hogan. Many golfers who took Hogan's words to heart and refused to examine them carefully in light of their own attributes became a little lost after reading his book. Curt Sampson in his biography of Hogan wrote that, "As with any textbook, each page [of *Five Lessons*] required time to absorb. Those who expected a page-turner didn't like it," while "A more fundamental criticism held that the absorption of every fine detail...was not worth the effort." Those details made *Five Lessons* the dissertation it is, but many readers found them difficult to absorb and understand. Still, Hogan, a master of self-improvement, wrote a textbook that offers an organized blueprint for golfers willing to put in the time and effort to improve. It helps, as I say, to be acutely aware of your tendencies, of your sources of error.

I hope that this book has shed a new light on Hogan's theories and has made it easier for you to understand his ideas, to evaluate them in light of your own swing, and to incorporate his philosophy where it can be of most help to you. It is now up to you to adapt and modify, but not copy, this information, to suit your own game. Armed in this way, a good player can go on to play really first-class golf. The average golfer can indeed think of breaking 80. These goals are well within your grasp. Practice with a purpose, and persevere, so that you can entrust your swing to muscle memory. Then you can turn your attention to all the challenges you will face in golf, a most demanding sport that is also so much fun to play.

Watching Hogan swing, one thought, "That's right, that's how a golf swing should look." Just as Sam Snead's glorious, flowing swing was majestic, Hogan's was electric, bursting with energy as the clubhead struck the ball. Hogan's love for the game and pursuit of perfection motivated him to become one of the game's most distinguished analysts and players. What does it say of the man when, in the last few years of his life, as the pain in his legs grew so intense that he could hardly walk, he would hit balls and practice at his beloved Shady Oaks Country Club in Fort Worth, Texas with the same focus and determination that he had in his youth? His quest for perfection and the exhilaration he felt from hitting solid shots never ended and stories of his ball-striking prowess are folklore in the golfing fraternity. As Hogan famously said, "Every day you don't hit balls is one day longer it is going to take you to get better."

Hogan was a man apart, a golfer who relentlessly pursued an answer to the abiding questions of the swing: What is the most reliable way of gaining precision and power? What can a human being do to approach the goals of consistency and reliability? Is there one way to swing the golf club that should supersede all other ways because it is better than all other ways?

Golfers who were interested in these questions, and even non-golfers who were fascinated by Hogan, followed him closely. I mentioned earlier how Larry Nelson started to play golf when he was twenty-one years old and learned to play from *Five Lessons*. I have also referred to Gardner Dickinson, the well-known player during the 1960s on the American tour. He studied Hogan intensely, so deeply did he believe in his methods. Dickinson wore a flat white cap, like Hogan, and tried to emulate him in many other ways, not the least of which was his swing. Hogan took it upon himself to work with Dickinson, and helped him improve his swing. His contemporaries called Dickinson a "mini-Ben." Dickinson once told the Canadian golfer George Knudson (another fierce Hogan disciple who modeled his swing after Hogan's and who had a reputation as a marvelous ball-striker) something very interesting. He said that Hogan felt there were only about five things that could go wrong in his swing, and

that he used these checkpoints when he practiced. However, Hogan also told Dickinson that he never had to go past two checkpoints to make the correction. Knudson said that Hogan could put his finger right on the problem because he knew his swing so well. Hogan had painstakingly constructed his swing to meet the demands of championship golf.

Knudson won eight times on the PGA Tour, and had the good fortune to play with Hogan eleven times in tournaments one year during the course of a few weeks. Knudson, in an unpublished manuscript, once related the following observations to the Canadian journalist Bob Moir: "It was particularly difficult to play golf with Hogan," Knudson said. "I felt like a spectator. This was no different than the feeling of dozens of other players. I've heard many a guy on tour say he felt he should be caddying while Hogan was around. He was so great in my eyes it was almost embarrassing to play with him. He was perfection. I always felt I should be home practicing, trying to create something, rather than trying to compete against him with what I had going for me. He always made me feel I was out of my class. He often made me wonder what in hell I was doing on the tour. I can honestly say I've never felt the same with anybody else. I didn't care who it was. If they wanted to play, I was ready to play. But Hogan was that far above everybody else. When Hogan was around I just stood and watched. I used to tell my caddie, 'Watch, this guy is really going to hit a shot here.' It was a challenge to tell my caddie what shot Hogan was going to hit and then see him execute it exactly that way."

Hogan remains a towering figure in the game. Writers have often tried to come to grips with who he was and with what made him so dedicated to solving the mysteries of the swing. Pat Ward-Thomas was an English writer who was a Hogan aficionado, and a man who knew genius when he encountered it. He wrote a piece in the *Guardian* newspaper in October of 1965 under the title "Hogan Loves

Hogan's calloused hands tell the story of his practice habits.

Golf as Few Have Done." In this piece Ward-Thomas captures the essence of the man, or comes as close as possible when considering somebody as complex as Hogan.

"Hogan remains aloof, seemingly scornful of adulation, cheap, easy familiarity and publicity," Ward-Thomas wrote. "He allows his colossal record, still the mightiest of his generation, to speak for itself, believing that his form of expression was solely through playing the game. This was his life; all else was secondary in the quest for perfection; no one ever pursued the ultimate in technical achievement with greater intensity."

The endless hours during which Hogan hit balls provided immense pleasure for him. He was insatiable in pursuit of a better way. "I got the greatest satisfaction from practicing," he said. "There is no greater pleasure than improving. The fellow who is a 90 shooter and shoots 87 experiences the same enjoyment as the fellow who goes from 70 to 69. That's what makes golf such a great game." Hogan eventually unearthed a fundamentally sound method which stood up, for him, to the pressure of tournament play. His dedication to hitting thousands of balls is not for everyone, and not only because of time constraints. Hogan really enjoyed hitting balls, and not every golfer does. Combine his work ethic, his incisive mind, his absolute concentration and his steely resolve on the golf course (the Scots nicknamed him the Wee Ice Mon at Carnoustie when he won the British Open there in 1953) and you have the complete golfer.

Hogan's practice habits are a wonderful legacy to all golfers. He was very systematic, and liked to hit balls in twenty-minute sessions, then take a short break. He worked hard on every ball he hit, on every shot he hit. Hogan did not just beat balls: *he practiced.* He advocated that the golfer interested in improving his methods should work thirty minutes a day at home on such elements as grip, stance, and swing plane. Hogan did a lot of mirror

practice, fixing images in his mind's eye while doing so. His practice was much more than hitting balls; when he was practicing without a ball he was still helping himself build up muscle memory so that when he did hit the ball it was with more instinct and less conscious effort. Hogan loved to hit balls to a caddie; something surely went out of the game when, at tournaments, the practice of professionals hitting balls to their own caddies was stopped. Hogan liked nothing better than to spend his time alone on the range, hitting balls to a caddie, working the ball left to right, right to left, high, low, controlling the distance—using his imagination and feel as if he were on the course.

Another part of Hogan's legacy is that he showed us one can play top-level golf for many years; he won three majors in one year—1953—when he was forty. Similarly, we can look to the current superstar senior Hale Irwin, and to Mark O'Meara, who at age forty-one in 1998 won the Masters and the British Open, and, of course, Jack Nicklaus, who in 1986 won his sixth Masters when he was forty-six. Certainly Hogan's putting deteriorated as he got older, and he thought of putting as "a game within a game" that was not worthy of being considered equal to the rest of the game. He said that a putt should count as only half a shot. A number of people have said that Hogan was driven nearly to despair when paired with the legendary South African Bobby Locke, one of the finest putters in the history of the game.

And yet Hogan was a far better putter than people, or even he himself, gave him credit for. He worked quite diligently on his putting, contrary to popular opinion. Prior to the Masters one year he was practicing in Florida when he played a round with Cary Middlecoff, who won two United States Opens and one Masters. Hogan used a split-handed grip that round and holed everything on his way to shooting in the low 60s. Soon after that round, Middlecoff and Hogan played a practice round at the Masters. Middlecoff noticed on the first green that

Hogan had reverted to his normal grip and asked why he wasn't using the split-handed grip with which he had so much success. "I couldn't bring myself to do that in front of all these people," Hogan answered. He was a purist.

Hogan will always be known for his ball-striking. It is revealing of the place he thought putting should have in the game, not to mention how little he thought he could offer in the way of instruction about it, that Hogan did not include a chapter on the subject in *Five Lessons*. Still, Hogan was a phenomenal putter from ten feet and in. Bob Rosburg told me he was one of the best holer-outers from that range; Byron Nelson said that Hogan could go weeks without missing a three-footer. No wonder he shot so many low scores. He capitalized on his precise iron play.

It really was a shame that Hogan did not play the emerging senior tour in its formative years, as did Sam Snead, Tommy Bolt, and others. He felt that if he could not play up to his ability he did not want to play—such was the character of the man. And yet it's amazing to think that, although he left serious competitive golf by the late 1950s, even today one finds so-called "Hogan clones." They wear his cap, his white shirt, gray pants, and black shoes, and hope to find a swing plane to match. Hogan is still a part of the golfing scene. He always will be.

Hogan in *Five Lessons* said he wrote down in a simplified manner all his thoughts from twenty-five years of playing and practicing. Or did he give us only part of the story and force the reader to read between the lines? If so, was he teasing us to dig deeper, not only into his writing but also into the ground on the practice range to learn about the swing in our own ways? We will never know.

What we do know is that Hogan felt it was every golfer's obligation to experiment and to find out for himself what worked best for him. Hogan wanted us to understand unequivocally that a few fundamentals are critical. But he did not want any golfer to have everything given to him; he didn't have everything—or much of anything—given to him. I have tried to offer some insights into Hogan's work and, I hope, to simplify things in a way that will help golfers understand Hogan's ideas more clearly.

Hogan grew up in tough times and made it through sheer desire and perseverance. His character was such that even the media considered him a tough nut. Henry Longhurst, the much-admired British writer and golf analyst, wrote a piece about Hogan that he called "A Hard Case from Texas." The piece appeared in 1957. Hogan was a hard case all right. Stories abound about young tour players visiting him to see if they could glean some advice; invariably they would say that they felt somewhat snubbed. I always think in this context of that famous story of Gary Player calling up Hogan and saying "Mr. Hogan, I wonder if I could ask you for some advice," and Hogan asking Player, "Do you play Ben Hogan clubs, son?" "No, I play Dunlop clubs, sir." "Well, then," Hogan answered briskly, "call Mr. Dunlop."

Hogan drove himself. He put his swing under a microscope, concluded it was lacking, and then set about to recalibrate and rebuild every element of how he went about the business of striking the golf ball. In doing so he developed what had to be one of the strongest golfing minds ever seen. He was not a big man, as I have said, and so he needed an edge. Hard work—driving, ferocious hard work—would provide his first edge. And this would unlock what Longhurst decided was his sharpest edge: that golfing mind.

"Coldly and deliberately Hogan decided he would find an edge by superior powers of concentration," Longhurst wrote. "The process took some years, but he did it. He got his mind into such a condition that nothing, neither idiotic spectators, nor unlucky breaks, nor the trembling thought of 'this for $5,000,' nothing, ever, would put him off, nothing prevented him playing at crucial moments the same sort of shots he could so easily unloose on the practice ground."

It can all appear so cold, can't it? But under Hogan's frosty exterior burned a desire so hot that he achieved immortality in golf. Many people have said it's a pity he wasn't more open and outgoing, that he should have given much more back to the game. But he did give back to the game; his gift, I think, was his reticence. He showed us that the individual golfer alone on the practice tee can learn about himself and the swing. He showed us that it is possible to find lasting satisfaction on the range and ultimately on the course. It's true that Hogan was somewhat secretive and aloof. One thing is sure, though: the game has been richer by far for having Hogan as one of its heroes. Jack Nicklaus said it all after Hogan's death in 1997: "I think we've lost the best shot-maker the game has ever seen."

And what of the future? Hogan wrote in *Five Lessons* that advances would be made, and they have.

The advances have come in analyzing the details of the swing by using video and computers, and in communication; teachers are able to convey information in a simpler and more readily identifiable manner. Biomechanics,

the mental side, fitness, and precision club fitting will all play a big part in the future of the game. Highly skilled young athletes will come into the sport, hitting the ball miles. And yet golf will remain a testing, tormenting game for most players, one where human nature will still get into the mix and, perhaps, interfere with progress by reaching for the quick-fix approach, the tip, the new driver. It's the nature of the game as well as the nature of the human being. It's been that way since the game began and I hope it never changes. I would love it if non-golfers the world over could learn about the fascination and the mystery of this endlessly stimulating game and have the opportunity to pursue their newfound interest. Hogan found it fascinating all his golfing life. I have also found it fascinating, truly an endless study and journey to which each and every golfer can contribute, and in which all golfers can participate. Every golfer can, in learning from the past, find his own path to follow. That path will lead to more questions, and will mean that the quest continues.

And that, I think, is the beauty of a beautiful game, a game in which the name Ben Hogan will always be synonymous with purity—the purity of his vision, and the purity of the way he struck the golf ball.

# BEN HOGAN

**born** August 13, 1912, Stephenville, Texas

**married** April 14, 1935, Valerie Fox

**died** July 25, 1997, Ft. Worth, Texas

---

## TOURNAMENT VICTORIES, ACHIEVEMENTS, AND HONORS

**1938**
Hershey Four-Ball

**1940**
North and South Open
Greensboro Open
Asheville Open
Goodall Round-Robin
Vardon Trophy Winner
Leading Money Winner, $10,655

**1941**
Miami Four-Ball
Asheville Open
Inverness Four-Ball
Chicago Open
Hershey Open
Vardon Trophy Winner
Leading Money Winner, $18,358
U.S. Ryder Cup Team Member

**1942**
Los Angeles Open
San Francisco Open
Hale America Open
North and South Open
Asheville Open
Rochester Open
Vardon Trophy Winner
Leading Money Winner, $13,143

**1945**

Nashville Open
Portland Open
Richmond Open
Montgomery Open
Orlando Open

**1946**

Phoenix Open
Texas Open
St. Petersburg Open
Miami Four-Ball
Colonial National Invitation
Western Open
Goodall Round-Robin
Inverness Four-Ball
Winnipeg Open
PGA Championship
Golden State Championship
Dallas Invitational
North and South Open
Vardon Trophy Winner
Leading Money Winner, $42,556

**1947**

Los Angeles Open
Phoenix Open
Miami Four-Ball
Colonial National Invitation
Chicago Open
Inverness Four-Ball
International Championship
U.S. Ryder Cup Team Member and Captain

**1948**

Los Angeles Open
PGA Championship
U.S. Open
Motor City Open
Western Open
Inverness Four-Ball
Reading Open
Denver Open
Reno Open
Glendale Open
Bing Crosby Pro-Am
Vardon Trophy Winner
Leading Money Winner, $32,112
Player of the Year

**1949**
Bing Crosby Pro-Am
Long Beach Open
U.S. Ryder Cup Team Captain

**1950**
Greenbrier Invitational
U.S. Open
Player of the Year

**1951**
Masters
U.S. Open
World's Championship
U.S. Ryder Cup Team Member
Player of the Year

**1952**
Colonial National Invitation

**1953**
Masters
Pan-American Open
Colonial National Invitation
U.S. Open
British Open
Player of the Year
Inducted into USPGA Hall of Fame

**1959**
Colonial National Invitation

**1965**
Named greatest player of all time by U.S. golf writers

**1967**
U.S. Ryder Cup Team Captain

**1974**
One of thirteen inaugural inductees to the World Golf Hall of Fame

**1976**
Bobby Jones Award Winner

133